CREATIVE BIBLE STUDY METHODS

Visualized for Personal and Group Study

By
RAY E. BAUGHMAN

Illustrated by
LARINDA SKAGGS

MOODY PRESS
CHICAGO

This book is dedicated to the students
in my Bible Study Methods class
at Dallas Bible College.

© 1976 by
THE MOODY BIBLE INSTITUTE
OF CHICAGO

ISBN: 0-8024-1635-7

Library of Congress Cataloging in Publication Data
Baughman, Ray E.
  Creative Bible study methods.

  Bibliography: p. 127
  1. Bible—Study. I. Title.
BS600.B34   220'.07   76-46625
ISBN 0-8024-1635-7

Contents

A Special Note to the Student

Many people can drive a nail and saw a board, but this doesn't mean that they can build a cabinet or some other piece of fine furniture. They may bend the nail, or saw crookedly, so they must learn to master the basic skills before they can be expected to combine them in such a complex project.

Analytical study of a Bible book can be compared to such a project, for basic Bible-study skills must be mastered before such a study can be completed. This book is designed to develop the required skills so that the student can learn to do analytical Bible book studies as well as use other methods that require special skills.

Creative approaches have been used to introduce the student to these skills, but in most cases the emphasis should be upon the skills and not the methods. While it is my hope that the creative approaches will capture the student's imagination and interest, many of the first methods will be used only a few times. But if the skills are learned and practiced, they can be used throughout a lifetime of study.

INDIVIDUAL OR GROUP STUDY

This book can be adapted for use in Sunday school, a training hour, home Bible classes, vacation Bible school, retreats or camps, or for individual study. If you have the opportunity, the first ten chapters can be used in any order and by themselves. You do not need to have a series of lessons. Chapter 17 includes programmed instruction on the use of *Young's Analytical Concordance to the Bible*. You can complete it at any time or after chapter 12.

To aid in group study, you have permission to reproduce the charts in this book. With a little effort, you can make attractive drawings on a mimeograph stencil, spirit master, or offset master, which will help create a good atmosphere of interest.

TWO STUDY SCHEDULES

Systematic study practiced over a few months will accomplish a lot. Two schedules are presented in this book. If you follow the weekly schedule, by the time you have finished this book you will have studied the books of 1 and 2 Timothy. They are chosen because they contain so much practical help for a young Christian who wants to serve the Lord and to live for Him.

If you follow the daily schedule (using one chapter a week), you will have read and studied 1, 2, and 3 John, James, Jude, Philemon, Titus, 1 and 2 Thessalonians, Philippians, Galatians, Mark, and assignments in John, 1 Peter, Proverbs, and Psalms. The last two weeks will be spent in doing an analytical study of the book of Colossians. You will have made your own personal commentary, something which not one Christian in 10,000 will ever do. But the most important thing is what it will do to your heart. "But we all, with open face beholding as in a glass the glory of the Lord, are changed into the same image from glory to glory, even as by the Spirit of the Lord" (2 Co 3:18).

Introduction

Most people feel that they should study the Bible more than they do. But they are not satisfied with their ability to study it because they feel that for the time and effort they put in, they should get more out of it. Often they lack confidence in their interpretations, so they take the lazy way out by depending upon others to explain it for them. They would resent being called spoon-fed Christians, but that is actually what they are.

This book is based upon five basic premises:
1. God means for you to study the Bible.
2. You can study the Bible for yourself.
3. You can enjoy this study.
4. You can experience or put to use the things you study.
5. You can share the things you study with others.

The methods used in this book are controlled by four principles:
1. *One of the ministries of the Holy Spirit of God is to teach, guide, and instruct the Christian.* Who could know more about His Book than the Author? (Jn 14:17, 26; 16:13). You must constantly rely upon His help.
2. *Bible study is a skill.* Like any other skill, it must be learned, so it will take work and practice. The most efficient and practical way to learn a skill is to break it down into small steps or parts. Some of the study methods suggested are of a very temporary variety and are meant to be practiced only a few times.
3. *Most Bible study should ultimately be related to Bible book study.* This insures that the interpretations will not be out of context. Consequently, by the time you finish

7

this book, you will have been introduced to numerous Bible-study skills, but they will be brought together so you can know how to do an analytical study of a book of the Bible and be able to write your own personal commentary if you want to.

4. *Studying the Bible with others can be mutually beneficial.* Ephesians 4 teaches that Christians should minister to one another and build one another up through the exercise of their spiritual gifts. This book and the methods advocated within it can be used advantageously in a group or class. In this way you can compare and share your work and ideas. After the methods are learned, you can go "on your own." Even then, the real joy will come as you use or share the fruit of your study in your Christian ministry.

Will you accept the challenge and be obedient to the command of God? "Study to shew thyself approved unto God, a workman that needeth not to be ashamed, rightly dividing the word of truth" (2 Ti 2:15). If so, you have the promise of His divine resources: "All scripture is given by inspiration of God, and is profitable for doctrine, for reproof, for correction, for instruction in righteousness: that the man of God may be perfect, throughly furnished unto all good works" (2 Ti 3:16-17). In other words, you will have all you need to be a mature ministering Christian.

THREE BASIC STUDY GOALS

Bible-study methods are not an end in themselves. If they were, they would be only "busywork." But three valid basic study goals can be named: (1) know what the Bible *says*; (2) know what the Bible *means*; and (3) know how to use or *apply* what it says.

These should not be considered three steps, because they do not necessarily follow in sequence. It is better to consider them as areas and to realize that they often overlap. Different study methods will help fulfill one or more of these areas or goals, but the purpose will not be to classify or demonstrate

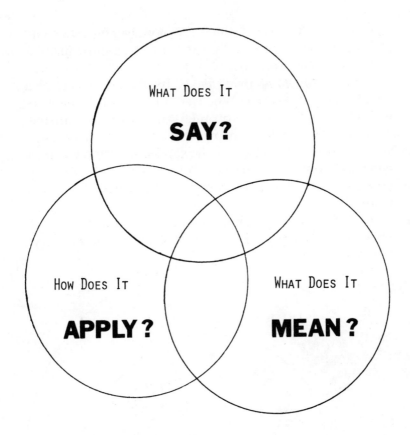

WHAT DOES IT

SAY?

HOW DOES IT

APPLY?

WHAT DOES IT

MEAN?

Fig. 1   Three Basic Study Goals

these three goals but, rather, to accomplish the overall goal of obtaining a usable and accurate knowledge of the Bible. (See fig. 1.)

1. *Know what it says.* You will do preliminary surveys and detailed studies of the text by using reference works, other translations, and commentaries to help you understand exactly what the text says and to develop your power of observation.

2. *Know what it means.* After looking at the text in detail, you will be introduced to various methods to help you master its content in a meaningful way. The goal is to help you

understand it. Certain methods are more helpful with some chapters than with others. Remember that no single method will serve in all instances.

3. *Know how to apply or use it.* Bible study should be a life-changing experience. When it is not, it is only an intellectual exercise that leads to pride rather than to Christian maturity. The application of Bible truth should follow a specific order. First, it should be applied to your own life or people will say, "Practice what you preach" or "I hear what you are saying but your actions speak louder than your words."

But what you are learning should not stop with yourself. How can you apply this truth to your Christian ministry? (See fig. 2.)

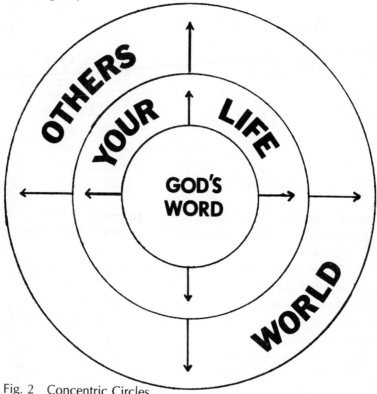

Fig. 2   Concentric Circles

This application of truth to life can be made in both unstructured and structured methods. Unstructured application refers to ideas, thoughts, exhortations, reproofs, and directions that can readily be seen or understood in studying the text without an application step.

Structured application refers to sermons, lessons, devotionals, or messages that make direct applications to life through illustrations or direct appeals.

SUGGESTIONS FOR THE TEACHER

It is much easier to teach someone the Bible than to teach him how to study the Bible for himself. Most people who consistently practice independent Bible study will tell you that somehow they learned "on their own." They can give suggestions but usually have a difficult time teaching others.

Many books have been written on Bible study methods. Some are too complicated. They give a beautiful example of a method and then say, "Go thou and do likewise." But the student needs to be taken step-by-step through the study. Often there are so many things the student is supposed to know or do that he is like a juggler who has five oranges in the air and feels like they are all about to fall on his head.

This text tries to avoid some of the difficulties (1) by giving step-by-step instructions and concentrating at first upon individual skills, (2) by directing attention on the specific skill rather than the general method, and finally (3) by relating skills to one another and to the analytical study of a Bible book.

As an instructor, some of your most important tasks will be motivation, encouragement, and clarifying goals. It is important to keep emphasizing to the class that they are learning *skills* which will help them meet their Bible study goals of (1) What does the Bible *say?* (2) What does it *mean?* (3) How does it *apply?* Remind them that by the end of the book they will be *applying the skills* to the analytical study of a Bible book.

The purpose of this section is to give you additional suggestions in teaching the methods. Remember, you need to show your enthusiasm concerning the importance of personal Bible study. But you want them to study, so don't do the work for them. Always try to commend a sincere effort; don't be too critical. False doctrine needs to be corrected, but many times it is a communication problem. Sometimes you can say, "That's good, but we need to say it in a different way so it won't be misunderstood."

MEET SMA
(pronounced Sammy)

Little "Sammy" wants to remind you of your basic study goals. He will help keep you in meaningful and profitable Bible study rather than intellectual tangents that are unprofitable.

The "S" is used to make his head; listen to what he *says*. The "M" is used for his torso or the area of his heart. "What is the heart *meaning* of the passage?" Feet are added to the "A." You put the passage to work by *applying* it. (See fig. 3.)

Fig. 3   Meet SMA

HEART-CHECK BIBLE STUDY

Bible Ref. _I Thes. 1:1-10_

E. K. G.
−(Heart moved)+

Verse	Diagnosis and Observations (Why?)
1.	God gives peace
2.	Priviledge of intercessory prayer
3.	{ Work of faith – our work is important, eternal results Labor of love - not just duty Patience of hope – endurance because of hope of Christ's coming. God is watching
4.	God chose us
5.	Want ministry to be in the power of the Holy Spirit – importance of a good testimony
6.	Holy Spirit can give joy even during afflictions
7.	Be a good example
8.	What a small group can do
9.	God is alive and true, not deceitful Jesus is coming again
10.	He saved us from the judgment to come
11.	

Prescription (What are you going to do about it?)

Spend more time in prayer
Rely upon the Holy Spirit's help as I teach
next Sunday.

14

1

Heart-Check Bible Study

You need to be encouraged and shown at the very start that you can study the Bible and enjoy it. The Bible can speak to your heart.

Normally a passage of about ten verses will make a good portion to study. It should cover a logical division of Scripture and can vary a few verses more or less if necessary. A chapter can be studied but it is often too long for the amount of time you can spend in a class.

Step 1. Using the heart in a spiritual sense, this study is designed to allow you to use the Bible to check your heart. First, look at the graph on the left side of the chart. It represents an EKG (electrocardiogram) that is used to check the human heart. The numbers down the page represent the verses in the passage you are studying. If it is John 1:10-18, you would put 10-18 rather than 1-11. To use the graph, read through the passage you are studying verse by verse. This will give you a preliminary survey. After reading each verse, put a dot on the graph next to the verse number. The more you are impressed by the content of the verse, the closer to the plus side you will place your dot. Everyone's graph will be a little different because you are to record, "How does this verse speak to me?"

You need to be honest. Every verse will not just "thrill" you; but on the other hand, if none impresses you or moves you, you might be "spiritually dead" or very sick. Not over thirty seconds should be spent making this judgment after you have read the verse. If you take longer, you are missing the point of this step, which is a preliminary survey to familiarize you with the passage and to make you observant and require you to begin to interact with what you have read.

It may move you or speak to your heart because of a desire, a precious promise, a command, a word of comfort, a conviction of sin, or a need in your life. So it is not as important in this step to ask "why" it speaks to you as it is to know that it does. After reading through the passage and placing your dots on the graph, connect the dots so that you have a graph line.

Step 2. Go back over the passage verse by verse and explain why it spoke to your heart. You will not necessarily have a comment on every verse, for you are now making your observations and diagnosis. On the second reading you may wish to make observations that you didn't notice on the first preliminary survey. This is encouraged.

If you are in a class, you will usually want to stop after making observations on about five verses and share your observations and diagnosis with one another. For some who may be having trouble getting things down on paper, this will be very helpful. Usually in the first attempt you will find that you are trying to be too profound in the observations. It is always interesting to see the variety of observations a group of people will make from the same passage. Normally you will want to allow two to three minutes per verse for independent study. After everyone has had an opportunity to share, repeat this procedure on the remainder of the passage.

Step 3. This step is the prescription. God has spoken to your heart through His Word. What are you going to do about it? This is to be a personal prescription, so it should be written in the first person singular and based upon the passage you have been studying. For example, "I need to be more considerate of my brother_____." Or, "I must not go to (this place) where I know I will be tempted to (sin)."

16

If the applications are not too personal, the group should be encouraged to share their prescriptions with one another. It is interesting to note that after a passage has been studied, especially by a group, if a person is asked to make a new graph line on his EKG, it will almost always be higher. More verses will speak to him and usually they will speak more intensely. This is as it should be.

PURPOSE OF THE HEART-CHECK BIBLE STUDY

You will probably want to do this type of study only about half a dozen times. You should have made some progress in the developing of your skills of observation by asking, "What does it say?" and "What does it mean?" You also have gained some practice in writing down your observations. But the big progress should have been made in the area of personal application, "How does it apply to me?" The purpose as expressed in 1 Thessalonians 3:13 is "To the end he may stablish your hearts unblameable in holiness before God."

SUGGESTED STUDIES:

Daily schedule	*Weekly schedule*
Sunday—John 13:1-10	1 Timothy 1:1-11
Monday—John 13:11-20	
Tuesday—John 13:21-30	
Wednesday—John 13:31-38	
Thursday—John 14:1-10	
Friday—John 14:11-20	
Saturday—John 14:21-31	

Each day write out a personal application from the material you are studying.

SUGGESTIONS FOR THE TEACHER

This first lesson is important. We want every individual to see that the Word of God can speak to his heart. No one should feel like he is under pressure, or that his work or answers are going to be ridiculed. The general tendency of the student is to feel very inferior. There is often a hesitancy about sharing observations. This is because he feels that what he says should be some "profound" theological truth. We want to dispel this attitude quickly.

If you can create an atmosphere of interest at the beginning of each class, it will help set the mood. Use your creativity. We are going to talk about checking the heart. You might bring some kind of electrical meter to class (an electrician's volt meter would work). Explain that we don't have an electrocardiograph machine, but ask, "If this meter could register the actions of your spiritual heart when you study the Bible, what would it read?" A doctor's stethoscope (or even a toy) could also be used, but this would change the illustration a little.

Follow the directions in the chapter as to the interval of time for each step. If this is a weekly class, challenge them to do the studies given under the daily schedule. The important thing is to get them to *work on their own*. Explain that this first study is just a temporary method and review its purposes with them.

Remember, your main job is to *motivate* and *encourage*.

Slogan _Follow-up the Followers_

Bible Ref. _I Thes. 2_
(paragraph)

Subject _Ministering to new Christians_
(theme)

Object _Paul reminds them of how he ministered_
(purpose) _to them. They are to follow his example._

Action _Walk worthy of God v. 12_
(what is commanded) _Be bold v. 2. Please God not man v. 4. Be gentle v. 7. Speak truth Vs. 3, 7, 13. Be a good example v. 10. Exercise a fatherly care v. 11. Work hard v. 9._

Profit _I need to give more loving care to_
(apply the soap) _the members of my Sunday school class. I need to remember that the way I minister is as important as what I do._

20

2

Soap Bible Study

One of the great benefits of studying the Bible is the cleansing effect the Word of God has upon the heart. Jesus said, "Now ye are clean through the word which I have spoken unto you" (Jn 15:3). Ephesians 5:25-26 explains that "Christ also loved the church, and gave himself for it; that he might sanctify and cleanse it with the washing of water by the word."

In this Bible study you will use the word *SOAP* as an acrostic, with each letter representing a word and a step in the study.

Step 1. Read through the passage. It can be a paragraph or a chapter this time. As you read, ask yourself, "What is the *s*ubject, or theme, of this passage?" Your subject will be of a general nature, so don't try to define it too closely in this step. If you were asked the subject of 1 Corinthians 15, the answer would be "resurrection"; or 1 Corinthians 13, "love." If you were studying John 15, some might say the subject is "the vine and the branch," but more accurately it would be "fellowship with Christ." The vine and the branch is the illustration that Christ uses to explain the relationship with Himself.

Step 2. In this step you should read through the passage again and try to determine, "Why is this subject mentioned? What is the *o*bject, or purpose, of this?" In 1 Corinthians 13 it is to show the importance of love and how even the most important spiritual gifts lose their value unless used with love. In 1 Corinthians 15 the certainty, order, manner, and time of the resurrection of Christians, or "the details of the resurrection," are explained. In John 15, fellowship or union with Christ provides for cleansing, growth, fruitfulness, and blessing. In other words, "the benefits of union with Him." Sometimes it will be easy to state the purpose in a rather detailed way, but it is not necessary as long as you have the general idea.

Step 3. In almost every passage of Scripture, there will be commands, exhortations, or suggestions. It is important to determine to whom the passage is addressed. Genesis 7:1 says, "Come thou and all thy house into the ark." You can't do this, and besides, it was addressed to Noah. (You can make an application and come into the place of safety in Jesus Christ, but that is something different.) All the Bible was written *for* us, but not all of the Bible was written *to* us. Read through the passage and list any *a*ction, or commands, it contains that will apply to you as a Christian, such as: "Pray without ceasing" (1 Th 5:17); "Be strong in the Lord, and in the power of his might" (Eph 6:10); or "Be filled with the spirit" (Eph 5:18).

Step 4. Bible study should serve a useful purpose. Ask yourself, "What *p*rofit is there for me in this passage? How can I apply the soap to my life?" Both the purpose and commands must be considered. The profit should be written in the first person singular, for example: "I am going to set aside more time for prayer by regularly praying for my classmates as I walk to school each day." Or, "I will make it a point to consciously call upon the Lord when I am tempted to cheat in my studies." It is important to try to plan how you are going to put these decisions into action and when you are going to do so. If you don't, you are like the man described in James 1:22-24 who looked in a mirror and then went his own way and forgot what he saw. Be a hearer and a doer of the Word. It will often prove very valuable for a class to share and discuss how they can personally put into practice the

22

commands of Scripture and apply them to their day-by-day activities so they can profit from them.

Step 5. The final step is to write a slogan or title for the passage you have studied. It must not be too general, for it is to help you distinguish between this and other passages. It should not be too long or too hard to remember. Try to be creative. Think of yourself as an advertising man describing the contents and merits of this passage. It is also similar, in some ways, to writing a headline. It usually will include the subject or theme of the passage and state in some way the object or purpose. For example: "Use your gifts with T.L.C. (tender love and care)" (1 Co 13); "It's real—the resurrection" (1 Co 15); "The profit or loss in fellowship or nonfellowship" (Jn 15).

PURPOSE OF THE SOAP BIBLE STUDY

This type of Bible study has a limited use, so you won't need to do it many times. If you do it each day for a week, it should help you develop the skill of determining "What it says" and "What it means" as related to a passage as a whole. Detailed study skills will be developed later. Discerning a theme and purpose and describing them in a good title for the passage is a skill that you will use over and over. You should also have gained practice in making applications and developing a plan of action. In a class you will usually want to stop between each step and share your ideas.

SUGGESTED STUDIES

Daily schedule	*Weekly schedule*
Sunday—James 1:1-16	1 Timothy 1:12-20
Monday—James 1:17-27	
Tuesday—James 2	
Wednesday—James 3	
Thursday—James 4	
Friday—James 5:1-9	
Saturday—James 5:10-20	

Each day write out a personal application from the material you are studying.

SUGGESTIONS FOR THE TEACHER

One of the great needs felt by people all over the world is the need for cleansing from the defilement of sin. This is true of both the non-Christian and the Christian. The non-Christian will also have the burden of guilt upon him. The Christian will know that Christ has paid the penalty of sin in His work on the cross, yet he still will feel defiled by sin. Stress this in the introduction by using appropriate examples, perhaps from your personal experience, or by using an object lesson.

Bring a big bar of soap to class, or four bars with S-O-A-P printed on the wrappers. They can be used one at a time to indicate the four steps in our study.

Step four is important. Developing a plan of action is often a neglected step in the application of the Bible study. Have someone read to the class the passage in James 1:22-24.

For step five, ask your class to give some commercial slogans, for example, "DUZ does everything." See how many you can think of before you go to the spiritual slogans required in this study. A word of caution: Remember that you are trying to think of effective slogans for the topic that is under discussion. You don't necessarily want all the slogans to be related to soap nor do you want them to be just a modified form of some commercial slogan like, "He is the real thing." Think up unusual ways to state the message.

BIBLEGRAM

Briefly Tell the Message of this Passage: Paul is concerned about the Thessalonians' spiritual growth.

Bible Ref. I Thes. 3   Date A.D. 52

To: Christians at Thessalonica, Greece

Had to know how you're doing / Sent Timothy to help you / Didn't want suffering to hinder you / Timothy brought good news and your love / What a comfort and encouragement it was / We thank God and pray for your spiritual growth and ask Him to let us visit you /

From: Paul

Cost: $4400

26

3

Biblegram Bible Study

The telegram or cablegram uses as few words as possible to communicate the message. Some companies have developed their own code words, abbreviations, or slang to shorten the message because the cost of the telegram is determined by the number of words. The word "stop," which serves as a period, is free. The "Biblegram" method of study is an attempt to communicate the essential message in as few words as possible. Generally, you will have the tendency to include too many details.

Step 1. Read the passage all the way through. Usually a chapter can be used if it is not over twenty-five verses. Determine to whom the Biblegram is being sent and who is the sender. You may have to look back to the introduction of the book.

Step 2. Summarize the message. Usually, you will want to use one word for every four to five words in the text. Following telegraph style, eliminate all articles and other short words. Pretend that it is going to cost you $100 a word to send your Biblegram, but that you must get the message through.

Share your Biblegrams with one another. Count the cost of each. Who did the best job of communicating the message at the least cost?

Step 3. Reduce the Biblegram to one sentence and write it above the line.

Step 4. After studying the message of the Biblegram, decide what from it can be applied to your life. Write your response in a Biblegram back to God. Sign it personally, not as a class.

To: GOD

I will try to overcome afflictions in your strength. I desire to grow spiritually, be holy, and be mature when Jesus comes.

From:
SAM STUDYHARD

PURPOSE OF BIBLEGRAM BIBLE STUDY

All the Bible was written *for* us, but not all of the Bible was written *to* us. You must learn to see each passage in its context. A big difference exists between what God said to Israel and what He says to the Church, but it's all profitable (2 Ti 3:16). The summary gives you another opportunity to condense the passage to its basic message. Your Biblegram response is essentially a prayer of commitment after applying God's Word to your heart.

SUGGESTED STUDIES

Daily schedule
Sunday—1 John 1
Monday—1 John 2:1-17
Tuesday—1 John 2:18-29
Wednesday—1 John 3:1-10
Thursday—1 John 3:11-24
Friday—1 John 4
Saturday—1 John 5

Weekly schedule
1 Timothy 2

Each day write out a personal application from the material you are studying.

SUGGESTIONS FOR THE TEACHER

A telegram always seems to have a sense of importance attached to it. It is not used for casual correspondence; a letter will serve that purpose and be much less expensive. Try to assemble any materials that are related to this theme. You may be able to borrow a telegraph key from a ham radio operator or find a cap that looks like the kind that a delivery boy would wear.

A cap will be useful to emphasize that a delivery boy does

not change the message according to his whims but delivers it as he has received it. Your students should strive for accuracy when they write their summaries, shortening but not changing the basic message.

After the students have prepared their Biblegrams, pick out the best one. You may want to let the class vote on it. Find a place for it to be delivered, such as the opening exercises at Sunday school or as a part of the evening worship service. Use this opportunity to explain about the class and encourage others to participate in the Bible study.

After finishing this study, a challenge for the future might be in order. Have the students summarize a chapter a day for a month. Start with Matthew, as it can be finished in twenty-eight days. At the end of the month, summaries may be compared with one of the commentaries listed below. It is very encouraging to find that the Lord often shows us some of the same things that He showed the commentary author or that He has shown us new things. After the first month, the students may want to commit themselves to another month—or the rest of the year. A diary may be purchased from the variety store. Obtain one that has about a five-by-seven-inch page size and one page for each day. When finished, summaries will be bound and can be titled:

The Gospel of Matthew
as summarized by
Sam Studyhard

Can you imagine what it would do to one's understanding if this project were carried all through the Bible? It can be done in a little over three years. Not one person in a million has ever done this.

RECOMMENDED BOOKS

Morgan, G. Campbell. *An Exposition of the Whole Bible: Chapter by Chapter in one Volume*. Westwood, N. J.: Revell, 1959.

Lockyer, Herbert. *All the Books and Chapters of the Bible*. Grand Rapids: Zondervan, 1966.

FUNNEL BIBLE STUDY

Bible
Ref. _Heb. 12:1-2_
(paragraph)

Wherefore, seeing we also are compassed about with so great a cloud of witnesses, let us lay aside every weight and the sin which doth so easily beset us, and let us run with patience the race that is set before us.

Looking unto Jesus the author and finisher of our faith who for the joy that was set before him endured the cross, despising the shame, and is set down at the right hand of the throne of God.

Others are watching, so let us run to win, even as Jesus finished His Work.

Summarize
(About one
word for four)

Run the Race like Jesus.

Summarize the summary
(Like a headline)

"Pour it on me--"
(Application)
I must not let personal sin keep me from living for Christ. Things may be hard but it didn't stop Jesus and it shouldn't stop me.

"ME"

30

4

Funnel Bible Study

The Funnel Bible Study is designed to aid you in the study of a paragraph and to funnel it right down to where you live. It will help you see the basic message of the passage and apply it to your life.

Step 1. In the top circle of the funnel write the paragraph that is to be studied. In order to have room, you will probably have to write small. The very exercise of reproducing the text will help impress upon you "what" the passage says. Educators say that writing it out has the same value as reading it *eleven* times! If you are using this in a class and you have limited time, you may want to fill in this section before class, but everyone should be encouraged to try writing it out by hand at least once.

One of the requirements that God had for His king of Israel was to "write him a copy of this law in a book" (Deu 17:18). A king could have scribes prepare him a copy, but God said that he was to write his own. The Bible says that Christ has made us kings, so can we do less? (See Rev 1:6.)

Step 2. In the triangular section of the funnel you should summarize in your own words what the paragraph says. On an average, you should use about one word for every four or five of the text. It is only when you allow the Word of God to pass through your mind and then reproduce it in your own words that you will capture the meaning and determine the significance of the paragraph you are studying.

As an alternative for this step you may wish to outline the paragraph instead of summarizing it. Some paragraphs lend themselves to this treatment more readily than others. The average person will have more difficulty doing the outline than the summary.

Allow from five to seven minutes for each person to prepare his summary, and then let them share and discuss them with one another. The ability to rephrase the paragraph so that it includes the ideas and yet doesn't list all the details takes practice. It also calls for evaluation: What are the most important things in this passage?

Step 3. In the spout of the funnel you should summarize the summary. It can usually be one sentence and will be similar to a newspaper headline. In English composition classes, teachers will often ask the student to write or identify a topic sentence for a paragraph. This is similar, for it needs a subject and predicate.

Allow three to four minutes to summarize the summaries and then discuss them. Usually there will be one or two people who will have a unique way of saying things.

Step 4. The final step is the application. Your Bible study should be personal and profitable. First, apply it to yourself, *not* to the class. Let others do their own. Let any who will share their applications do so. This is usually the most exciting part of a class, because the number of different ways the Lord can use a passage in a class and meet so many personal needs is amazing.

PURPOSE OF THE FUNNEL BIBLE STUDY

This method should only be used a few times. Its purpose, however, is to develop in you the ability to see the essential core of truth in a passage. This skill is needed in doing analytical charts, making outlines, preparing devotionals, and developing a thesis for a sermon. It will also give you practice in making personal applications of the Scripture to your life.

SUGGESTED STUDIES

Daily schedule   *Weekly schedule*
Sunday—Titus 1:1-4   1 Timothy 3:1-7
Monday—Titus 1:5-9
Tuesday—Titus 1:10-16
Wednesday—Titus 2:1-8
Thursday—Titus 2:9-15
Friday—Titus 3:1-7
Saturday—Titus 3:8-15

Each day write out a personal application from the material you are studying.

SUGGESTIONS FOR THE TEACHER

Did you ever try to pour gasoline into your car without a funnel? If you have, you understand the problem of getting it to go where you want it to go. Bring a funnel to class. The bigger it is the better. Place a Testament or small Bible in the top. The problem is how to channel the truth and promises of the Bible into our hearts and lives.

In step two, the summary section, the tendency of many is to just enter a few key phrases or parts of the verses. Encourage the students to summarize the whole paragraph in their own words, words that are more inclusive. The translation of the material into their own language is important to their understanding. Educators consider this translation process as an important level of learning.

It is easy to make general applications of Scripture like "We Christians should be more definite in our praying." When students do this, you can say, "Oh-oh, you spilled some. Remember this is to be a personal application. How should you say that?" Of course, you want the student to change the application to, "I should be more definite in my praying."

Remind the class that when they give a devotional or teach a class, they can make applications for the group but in this study it is to be personal applications.

You may want to close this class session with the Scriptural example of Aaron the brother of Moses and High Priest of Israel. The holy anointing oil was placed on his head to consecrate him so that he could minister as a priest for the Lord (Ex 30:22-38). It ran down his head onto his beard and onto his garments (Ps 133:2). The application of the Word of God to our lives will make our lives a fragrance to others and prepare us to minister for God.

CLOCK BIBLE STUDY

REDEEMING THE TIME! (Eph. 5:16)

Bible Ref. _I Thes. 4:1-12_

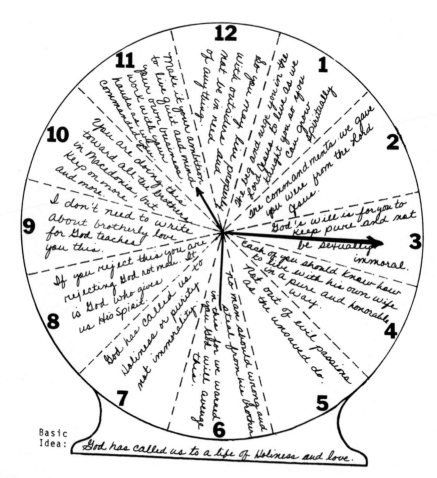

The clock contains handwritten text radiating from the center:

- So you may live in the with outsiders and not be in need of anything.
- We beg and urge you in the Lord Jesus to live as you can grow spiritually.
- The commandments we gave you were from the Lord Jesus.
- God's will is for you to keep pure and not be sexually immoral.
- Each of you should know how to live with his own wife in a pure and honorable way.
- Not out of evil passions as the unsaved do.
- No man should wrong and cheat from his brother, for we warned you like we will avenge this.
- God has called us to Holiness or purity, not immorality.
- If you reject this you are rejecting God not man. It is God who gives us His Spirit.
- I don't need to write about brotherly love for God teaches you this.
- You are doing this toward all the brothers in Macedonia, but keep on more and more.
- Make it your ambition to live quiet and mind your own business. Work with your hands as we commanded you.

Clock numbers: 12, 1, 2, 3, 4, 5, 6, 7, 8, 9, 10, 11

Basic Idea: God has called us to a life of Holiness and love.

SET THE HANDS
(on two most meaningful verses)
Big hand V. 3
Small hand V. 11

SET THE ALARM
(is there a warning?)
V. 6

36

5

Clock Bible Study

We should be "redeeming the time," Paul said in Ephesians 5:16, and one of the most profitable ways to invest time is in the study of the Word. In this lesson we are going to practice paraphrasing.

Step 1. The face of the clock is divided into sections. If you do not start with verse 1 in a passage, number the clock to fit the passage. Read through the passage under study, and then, verse by verse, write out a paraphrase of the verse in your own words as you understand the meaning.

This step can be done in two different ways, and you may want to try both. First, you could limit yourself to one translation and just practice studying what it says and then allow it to pass through your own mind and write it down in your own way of talking. Second, you can use commentaries and other translations to help you understand exactly what it is saying. Your paraphrase would then be more of an expanded translation, for you would try to capture all of the meaning that you could. Your style, in this case, will not be as smooth as in the first method.

In subsequent chapters you will be doing studies that will help you in the second method, so it is suggested that you use the first method at this time, and then you can try the second method later on your own, since it takes too much time for a class session. After you have completed about six verses, share your results with the class and then complete the paraphrasing.

Step 2. On the base of the clock, you are to write the basic teaching of the passage. It will be a one- or two-sentence summary of the passage. You must do this after you have studied the passage by paraphrasing it. The statement of the basic teaching should not be too detailed. Discuss this with each other in the class, and be ready to defend your statement with evidence from the text itself.

Step 3. This is a subjective step, and everyone can have his own opinions. Draw a big hand and a little hand on the clock's face and point them to the two most meaningful verses. In class, explain why they are meaningful to you, for example, because they contain a promise, a challenge, or a goal.

Step 4. In this step, set the alarm hand. Ask yourself, Is there a warning in the passage? It may be directly stated, or it may be something about which the Holy Spirit is speaking to you. If it isn't too personal, the class should share these warnings with one another.

PURPOSE OF THE CLOCK BIBLE STUDY

The new skill that this study teaches is to express what the Scripture says in your own words. You communicate it in the way you understand it using the best words possible. It will also cause you to interact with the Bible as you make personal judgments and applications by setting the hands of the clock.

SUGGESTED STUDIES

Daily schedule
Sunday—2 John
Monday—3 John
Tuesday—Jude 1:1-13
Wednesday—Jude 1:14-25
Thursday—Philemon 1:1-13
Friday—Philemon 1:14-25
Saturday—Proverbs 3:1-12

Weekly schedule
1 Timothy 3:8-16

(Combine two of the smaller verses, if necessary, to fit your chart.)

Each day write out a personal application from the material you are studying.

SUGGESTIONS FOR THE TEACHER

Time is valuable. We have only a limited supply (Ps 90). "So teach us to number our days, that we may apply our hearts unto wisdom" (Ps 90:12). As an object lesson, bring to class an alarm clock, sundial, hour glass (egg timer), wrist watch, pocket watch, and any other kind of time keeper you can find. The point we want to emphasize is that Bible study should have an important place in our time.

The skill of paraphrasing differs from the skill of summarizing that was practiced in the funnel study. In both cases the student tries to put the text in his own words. In a summary you try to communicate the basic truth in a condensed form, but in a paraphrase you use your own words as you understand it. After having completed a detailed study of the text, an expanded paraphrase will try to communicate all the details of the truth. You may even add extra words in brackets to try to explain all that it means.

A final challenge can be carried away from class by bringing a small-pointed felt-tipped marker to class (the washable kind). Ask the students to condense down to two or three words an exhortation from the lesson. Perhaps it will be from their best verse or alarm verse. "Be ready" (1 Pe 3:15), "Watch it" (the tongue, Ja 3:5), "Rejoice" (Phil 4:4), "Today?" (the Lord's return, 1 Th 4:16), or "With His help" (Phil 4:13). Use the marker to write this on the crystals of their wristwatches. Ask them to leave it there the next 24 hours. Every time they check the time they will be reminded of the Bible truth they studied.

If someone wants to know what is written on their watches, they can take it as an opportunity to tell him about the Bible study, about the Bible truth involved or as an opportunity to witness.

Why not make it a matter of prayer that God will use the message on the watch to open conversation with a heart that

He has prepared. If they ask the question, there should be no hesitancy on our part in sharing a spiritual message. This will really be buying up the opportunities.

PANEL DISCUSSION BIBLE STUDY

(Comparing Translations)

Topic: _Jesus is Coming Again_

Ref. _I Thes. 4:13-18_

KJV	NAS	AB	WT
13 But I would not have you to be ignorant, brethren, concerning them which are asleep, that ye sorrow not, even *as others which have no hope.	... be uninformed not grieve	asleep [in death] no hope [beyond the grave]	are falling asleep
14 For ʲif we believe that Jesus died and rose again, even so them also which sleep in Jesus will God bring with him.	about the same as KJV.	...then through Jesus asleep [in death]	through Jesus, God will bring with Him...
15 For this we say unto you ᵐ by the word of the Lord, that we which are alive *and remain unto the coming of the Lord shall not prevent them which are asleep.	— not precede	declare Lord's [own] word	on the Lord's own authority. — have no advantage
16 For ⁿthe Lord himself shall descend from heaven with a shout, with the voice of the archangel, and with the trump of God: and the dead in Christ shall rise first:	trumpet of God	loud cry of summons the shout of an archangel those who have departed this life	summons sounded by the archangel's call and by God's trumpet the dead in union with Christ
17 Then we which are alive *and remain shall be caught up together with them °in the clouds, to meet the Lord in the air: and so ᵖ shall we ever be with the Lord.	Always be	remain [on the earth,] shall simultaneously with (the resurrected dead) — through eternity of identity	with them on clouds in the air....
18 Wherefore ʳ comfort one another with these words.	Therefore ...	Comfort and encourage	Continue encouraging — with this truth

42

6

Panel Bible Study

Suppose you could pull your chair up to a table and join a group of Bible scholars in discussing the Scripture. Each one would be an expert in the original languages and would have studied various translations of the Bible. Each would be a specialist in his field and would have a certain audience in mind.

Actually, in our study each translation will represent a group of scholars. Even translations that are primarily the work of one person will represent the translator and his consultants. If this study is being done in a class, let one person be responsible for each translation. If you are doing it alone, get a big table so you can spread out all the translations around you.

Many translations are available today; some are much better than others. The following are suggested because of their value:

1. *The King James Version (KJV)*. This is still the most widely used English translation of the Bible. God has honored it for many years. But the English language has changed in the past 400 years, and it does have some difficult passages. Place this in the left-hand column and read it first.

2. *The New American Standard Bible (NASB)*. This is my favorite. It is being accepted by evangelical scholars and is likely to become a standard as time goes by. It is quite accurate.

3. *The Williams Translation (Williams)*. Charles B. Williams is especially recognized for his accurate translation of the Greek tenses. It is available only in the New Testament.

4. *The Amplified Bible (Amp.)*. This translation is more awkward to read, but it is very helpful in presenting the various meanings of words. Parentheses and dashes are used to include additional phrases of meaning. Brackets are used to contain clarifying words or comments. These may or may not be implied, but they are not actually expressed in the Greek text. These are the opinions of the translators and should be considered accordingly.

5. *The New International Version (NIV)*. This is an easy-to-read new translation by evangelical scholars. It supplies an accuracy that is sometimes lacking in modern translations.

6. *The Living Bible (TLB)*. You may want to use this; it is very popular. It is admittedly a paraphrase rather than a translation. In a paraphrase the author tries to translate the thought of the original but sometimes it will use an entirely different expression in order to give a clearer and fuller explanation in language that can be more easily understood. It is a joy to read and will often bring some new truth to your attention just because it is said in different words. You can honor this as the opinion of a conservative scholar in the same way you would value the opinion of a good Bible commentary.

RULES TO OBSERVE

Assuming that you do not know Hebrew or Greek (if you do place it in the left box), there are several rules that must be observed:

1. You must rely upon the Holy Spirit to guide you in your study. This is part of His ministry of teaching (Jn 14:26) and guiding believers (Jn 16:13).

2. The translation must be judged on the basis of the context of the passage.

3. The translation must be compared to the general teaching of Scripture. Is there a contradiction?

4. You are not to seek for variety just for the sake of variety. There are few words in one language that can be consistently translated by one word in another. For example, there is one Greek word that can mean either "spirit" or "wind." There are three different Greek words that are translated by the English word "life." Each has its own distinct meaning and the Amplified Bible usually brings this out.

5. The majority is not always right, but it should influence your thinking. If several agree, you should seriously consider it.

6. In your personal expanded translation or paraphrase, use brackets to enclose words or comments that are not actually in the text. In this way you can have a mixture of translation and commentary and still remember which is which at a later time. Always plan to preserve your work for your future use and ministry.

Step 1. Read the first verse in the King James Version, and then check each of the other versions in turn. If any version has a contribution to make toward rendering a word, phrase, or sentence more understandable or more meaningful, it should be considered. In the appropriate box write only the variations that you think are important. If it is about the same as the King James, you can write "same as KJV," or about the same as the New American Standard Bible, write, "same as NASB." In a class, discuss the various renderings.

Step 2. On a separate sheet of paper write out your personal expanded translation or paraphrase. Remember to put brackets around any comments or explanations that are not actually in the text. You can expect that your version will not flow as smoothly as regular translations, but it should be packed with special meaning for you. If you are studying in a group, share your translations.

Repeat steps one and two with each verse in the passage that you are studying.

Step 3. Read the entire passage through in your expanded translation. You now should have acquired an understanding of the passage that you didn't have when you began. Try to digest this understanding into a short title for the passage, and then write this title on the table above. This topic is what you and your experts have been discussing.

The following is an example of the Panel Bible Study:

PERSONAL PARAPHRASE OF 1 THESSALONIANS 4:13-18

13. I would not have you be uninformed, brothers, about those who are falling asleep [in death]; so you won't grieve as those who have no hope [beyond the grave].

14. For if we believe that Jesus died and rose again, then through Jesus, will God bring back those who have fallen asleep [in death].

15. For by the Lord's [own] Word, we declare that we which are alive and remain unto the coming of the Lord shall not have any advantage nor precede them which are asleep [in death].

16. For the Lord Himself will come down from heaven with a loud cry of summons, with the shout of an archangel, with the trumpet of God, and the dead in union with Christ will rise first.

17. Then we which are alive [upon the earth] will simultaneously with the resurrected dead be caught up in the clouds to meet the Lord in the air, and so we will always—through the eternity of eternities— be with the Lord.

18. So continue comforting and encouraging one another with this truth.

PURPOSE OF THE PANEL BIBLE STUDY

This type of Bible study should aid you in understanding what the Bible *says* and what it *means*. You will not necessarily use this form, but you should use the principle in any serious study of the Bible. The result will often be the same as using a commentary, but it has the advantage of keeping your attention on the Scripture itself.

SUGGESTED STUDIES

Daily schedule
Sunday—John 15:1-6
Monday—John 15:7-12
Tuesday—John 15:13-17
Wednesday—John 15:18-22
Thursday—John 15:23-27
Friday—John 16:1-7
Saturday—John 16:8-15

Weekly schedule
1 Timothy 4:1-6

Each day write out a personal application from the material you are studying.

SUGGESTIONS FOR THE TEACHER

For this Bible study you need to set the stage. Place a table at the front with four or five chairs. Have the participants all facing the audience if possible. Make a small sign to place in front of each panel member. They should be with letters about two inches high and fixed so they will stand up. You want the class to be able to read them.

You can select your panel members at the beginning of the class or well beforehand. As you introduce them, call them by the name of the version or the translator: King James, Mr. NASB (New American Standard Bible), Mr. Williams, Mr. Amp (Amplified Bible), Mr. Taylor (translator of *The Living Bible)*, Mr. NIV (New International Version), or whatever translations you use. These are the names on the signs and the names you address them by during the study.

Some verses deserve much more attention than others. Ask the panel to share any variation that they think is helpful. Do not just have each one read his translation in turn. Comments usually should be related to words and phrases more often than whole verses.

In the clock Bible study the paraphrase was based upon one translation. The emphasis was upon the process of paraphrasing. In this study, it is upon getting as complete a knowledge as possible on what the Bible says and means.

47

Be sure to leave some time for reading through the paraphrases that the students prepare.

If you have access to a photocopier, you can take an inexpensive King James Bible, clip the passage you plan to study, and paste it in the left hand margin of your work sheet. When you run this through the machine you have a nice copy to work from; in fact, it is better than a pasted-up original. A small New Testament works best because the lines are short and therefore it is easier to relate your notes to exact phrases and you have more room for your notes.

Any who have studied Hebrew or Greek could prepare personal study sheets for themselves. The important thing is to have notes that are uniform and of a quality that you can save for future study.

FILE BIBLE STUDY

(Cross References)

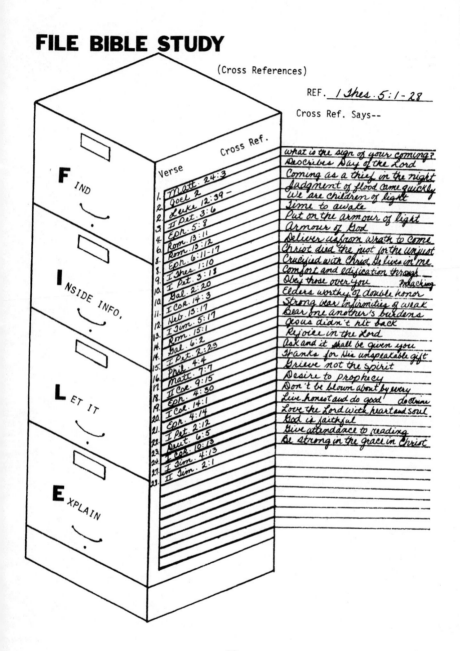

REF. _1 Thes. 5:1-28_

Cross Ref. Says--

FIND

INSIDE INFO.

LET IT

EXPLAIN

	Verse	Cross Ref.
		what is the sign of your coming?
		Describes Day of the Lord
1.	Matt. 24:3	Coming as a thief in the night
2.	Joel 2	Judgment of flood came quickly
3.	Luke 12:39 -	We are children of light
4.	II Pet. 3:6	Time to awake
5.	Eph. 5:8	Put on the armour of light
6.	Rom. 13:11	Armour of God
7.	Rom. 13:12	Deliver us from wrath to come
8.	Eph. 6:11-17	Christ died the just for the unjust
9.	I Thes. 1:10	Crucified with Christ He lives in me
10.	I Pet. 3:18	Comfort and edification through
11.	Gal. 2:20	Obey those over you teaching
12.	I Cor. 14:3	Elders worthy of double honor
13.	Heb. 13:17	Strong wear infirmities of weak
14.	I Tim. 5:17	Bear one another's burdens
14.	Rom. 15:1	Jesus didn't hit back
15.	Gal. 6:2	Rejoice in the Lord
16.	I Pet. 2:23	Ask and it shall be given you
17.	Phil. 4:4	Thanks for His unspeakable gift
18.	Matt. 7:7	Grieve not the spirit
19.	II Cor. 9:15	Desire to prophecy
20.	Eph. 4:30	Don't be blown about by every
21.	I Cor. 14:1	Live honest and do good! doctrine
22.	Eph. 4:14	Love the Lord with heart and soul
23.	I Pet. 2:12	God is faithful
24.	Deut. 6:5	Give attendance to reading
27.	I Cor. 10:13	Be strong in the grace in Christ
23.	I Tim. 4:13	
	II Tim. 2:1	

7

File Bible Study

The word *FILE* is an acrostic for this Bible study method. It stands for *F*ind *I*nside information. *L*et it *E*xplain. Every piece of information or spiritual truth that you learn from your Bible study will help you understand or explain new portions as you study. The Bible is its own best interpreter. It has this unusual feature: it explains itself more thoroughly than any other book does, often in the same passage. Many Bibles will have cross-references in the margins. You are encouraged to add your own to your Bible. Write them in neatly.

Parallel passages are those that speak of the same event or subject, that refer to another passage, or have some relationship. They can be divided into three kinds:

1. Parallels of words—love, temptation, life, shepherd.
2. Parallels of ideas (or incidents)—trust and faith (the same word is not necessarily used) or Jesus feeding the 5,000 (all four Gospels record this incident).
3. Parallels of general teachings—salvation is by faith, not of works; or God is all-powerful.

There are several sources where you can obtain these parallel references: the margin of your reference Bible, commentaries, or concordances. But the most profitable is through your own reading.

Step 1. Having selected a paragraph, look for a cross-reference that will explain some part of the first verse. List the number of the verse in the left-hand column. In this study try to find an average of at least one reference for each verse. For some, you may not be able to find any; and for others, you will find several.

Step 2. List the reference next to the verse number of the paragraph.

Step 3. Summarize in a phrase what the cross-reference says. What new fact do you see, or what way does it help explain the passage? What is its contribution? Unless it is a very familiar passage, you probably cannot remember it in a few months. Your work sheet should be a file of information and not a library card catalog that only tells you what to look up. Always record a note about what the verse says.

RULES FOR FINDING PARALLELS
OF WORDS OR EXPRESSIONS

Usually you will want to follow this order:
1. Look in the same book of the Bible.
2. Look in other books of the Bible by the same human author.
3. Look in other books written in the same time period.
4. Look in any Bible book.

PURPOSE OF THE FILE BIBLE STUDY

The Bible student needs to learn to let the Bible explain itself and to see the unity of its teachings. This skill will increase the more a student studies and becomes familiar with the Bible, but it is usually a very difficult task for the beginner. Later, it will be incorporated into other kinds of Bible studies. A half-dozen file studies may be done; they can be very rewarding.

SUGGESTED STUDIES

Daily schedule
Sunday—John 16:16-24
Monday—John 16:25-33
Tuesday—John 17:1-6

Weekly schedule
1 Timothy 4:7-16

Wednesday—John 17:7-12
Thursday—John 17:13-19
Friday—John 17:20-26
Saturday—Psalm 1

Each day write out a personal application from the material you are studying.

SUGGESTIONS FOR THE TEACHER

Bring a small file to class; a recipe file will do. Ask the class, "How much good would the file do me, if I dumped it on the table and mixed all the cards up? What if I really was not acquainted with the contents of the file or had used them very little?" The answer is obvious.

The *FILE* Bible study will begin to bring order to their knowledge of the Bible and give a better understanding of it. New Christians, because they are so unfamiliar with the Bible, often feel helpless. Start the students on parallels of words. Have them pick out what they consider to be an important word in a verse. If they have a small concordance in the back of their Bible, show them how to use it. You should bring to class another concordance, such as Young's, so it will be available. Remind them of the rules given in the textbook about finding parallel passages.

After they have practiced finding parallels of words, suggest they find a parallel of ideas. You may have to help by suggesting what to look for. Sometimes it is easier to see the relationship between verses if you are looking for parallels of ideas rather than of words. Some verses will use the same words but be totally unrelated.

It is easy to underestimate the difficulty that some people have finding cross references. Don't underestimate the rewarding feeling that finding a good parallel gives a new student.

WEATHER REPORT BIBLE STUDY

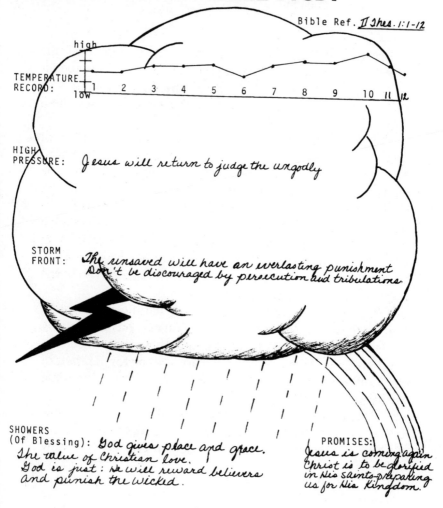

Bible Ref. _II Thes. 1:1-12_

TEMPERATURE
RECORD:

high

low   1   2   3   4   5   6   7   8   9   10   11   12

HIGH
PRESSURE: Jesus will return to judge the ungodly

STORM
FRONT: The unsaved will have an everlasting punishment
Don't be discouraged by persecution and tribulations.

SHOWERS
(Of Blessing):   God gives place and grace.
The value of Christian love.
God is just: He will reward believers
and punish the wicked.

PROMISES:
Jesus is coming again
Christ is to be glorified
in His saints—preparing
us for His Kingdom.

54

8

Weather Report Bible Study

Our feelings are often as changeable as the weather. Studying the Bible will help you have victory in stormy times as well as when the day seems sunny. Too often we look at circumstances rather than listen to Him who has control over circumstances.

Step 1. Read through the paragraph or chapter and then record your spiritual temperature, verse by verse. Are you hot or cold or lukewarm? Number your scale to match your verse numbers. This is to be a brief survey, so don't spend over half a minute on each verse.

Step 2. In the area of the cloud labeled "high pressure," state the basic subject of the passage. Try to condense it down to one sentence. It should contain not only the topic but what it is saying about the topic. You should allow three to four minutes for this step. Ask each one in your class to tell what he thinks it is and be ready to defend his answer from the text.

Step 3. Warning! Storm front approaching. Is there a warning in this passage, or has the Holy Spirit used this text to speak to you about something? Have those who are willing share this section with the class.

Step 4. Showers of blessing should come from studying the Word. Spend four to five minutes listing the blessings you have received from this passage, and then, if you are in class, share them with the others. If you are studying this alone, why not ask the Lord to make it possible for you to share the blessings of your study with someone, such as your family, your neighbor, or your fellow employee.

Step 5. God gave Noah the rainbow as a sign of His promise to never again destroy the earth with water, so in this study we are using the rainbow to represent God's promises. Are there any promises in this paragraph? Are they given to a certain individual or group, or are they universal promises? List the promise(s) and tell to whom they were given. If they apply to you, are you ready to claim them by faith? Can God be depended upon to keep His Word? Is He strong enough to be able to perform what He has promised?

PURPOSE OF THE WEATHER REPORT
BIBLE STUDY

There are two study skills that this method is designed to help you acquire. The first is to be able to get an overall grasp of a chapter. The second is to develop your powers of observation. You have been directed to look for three things: warnings, blessings, and promises. This method will only be used a few times, but the skills can be used in many ways in the study of the Word.

SUGGESTED STUDIES

Daily schedule
Sunday—1 Thessalonians 1
Monday—1 Thessalonians 2
Tuesday—1 Thessalonians 3
Wednesday—1 Thessalonians 4:1-12
Thursday—1 Thessalonians 4:13-18
Friday—1 Thessalonians 5:1-13
Saturday—1 Thessalonians 5:14-28

Weekly schedule
1 Timothy 5

Each day write out a personal application from the material you are studying.

SUGGESTIONS FOR THE TEACHER

Come to class wearing your raincoat and carrying an open umbrella. Everybody talks about the weather; few can predict it accurately; and even science can do little to change it. The Bible, however, can help us weather the storms of life, find the silver lining in the dark clouds, and rejoice in the showers of blessings.

This study introduces no new skills but does give additional practice to those studied in previous lessons, especially in the area of observations. It is easy to read without thinking.

This lesson can be used to associate Bible study with prayer in a different way by trying to limit the prayer to things studied or brought to mind by the study.

Encourage any who are waging spiritual battles (the storm fronts) to share them with the class, and then you should pray for one another. It is usually better to pray after each student than to wait and try to remember all the needs in one big prayer.

Praise the Lord for the "showers of blessing" that this study of the Word has brought to your attention. Suggest that a conversational prayer approach be used and a person mention only one blessing at a time. If he wants to give additional praise, he can do so after others have prayed.

It is a great challenge to claim the promises of God. We need to pray back to God, in faith, what He has promised. A word of warning, we should not misinterpret, misapply, or be presumptuous in claiming God's promises.

LADDER BIBLE STUDY

Bible Ref. _Rom. 4_

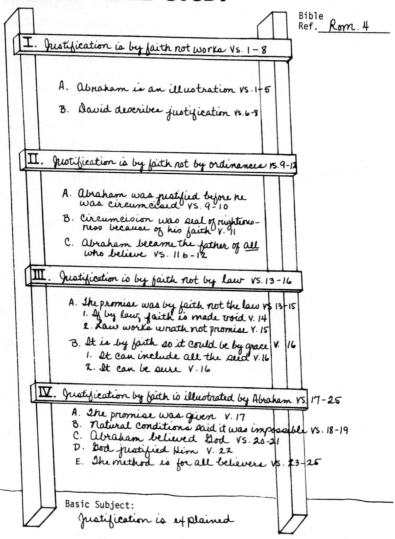

I. Justification is by faith not works vs. 1-8

    A. Abraham is an illustration vs. 1-5

    B. David describes justification vs. 6-8

II. Justification is by faith not by ordinances vs. 9-12

    A. Abraham was justified before he was circumcised vs. 9-10

    B. Circumcision was seal of righteousness because of his faith v. 11

    C. Abraham became the father of <u>all</u> who believe vs. 11b-12

III. Justification is by faith not by law vs. 13-16

    A. The promise was by faith not the law vs. 13-15
      1. If by law, faith is made void v. 14
      2. Law works wrath not promise v. 15

    B. It is by faith so it could be by grace v. 16
      1. It can include all the seed v. 16
      2. It can be sure v. 16

IV. Justification by faith is illustrated by Abraham vs. 17-25

    A. The promise was given v. 17
    B. Natural conditions said it was impossible vs. 18-19
    C. Abraham believed God vs. 20-21
    D. God justified Him v. 22
    E. The method is for all believers vs. 23-25

Basic Subject:

    Justification is explained

58

9

Ladder Bible Study

One of the most helpful abilities in understanding a chapter or passage is to be able to see the structure. Most people find outlining difficult. It is made more difficult because students are not usually taught to "discover" outlines. Rather, they are usually asked to outline their material before they write a paper or give a speech, but seldom are they told to analyze a paper or a speech for the outline. It is not difficult if approached by using the following steps:

Step 1. Read through the chapter or passage and try to answer, "What is the basic topic being discussed?" Is it love, temptation, giving, or discipleship? Try to express the subject of the passage in one or two words. Next, answer the question, "What does it say about that topic?" Love your enemies, resist temptation, giving should be an act of worship, or discipleship requires self-discipline. In other words, first decide what is the subject and then what is being said about the subject. It is usually helpful to go through this in a two-step process. Write this basic subject in the space at the base of the ladder. If you are studying as a class, share each step as you go along. There may be more than one major theme in a passage. The outline will, of course, be different for each theme. Some of the divisions may fall in the same place, but not necessarily all of them.

Step 2. If you are outlining a chapter, usually you can use the paragraph division as a preliminary guide. The original Greek and Hebrew manuscripts were not divided into verses or paragraphs, so you will find a difference of opinion among the editors of the various translations as to how the paragraphs should be divided. Some tend toward shorter paragraphs than others. After studying the text you may want to combine several short paragraphs or divide a long one. But first, read the paragraph and ask yourself, "What does this paragraph have to say about the basic topic?" It is not enough to just ask, "What is it saying?" It needs to be related to the basic topic.

Write your answer on the top rung of the ladder. If you are in a class, compare your answers.

Step 3. The verses in the paragraph should each have something to say about that rung (paragraph title) of the ladder. In the space below the rung, summarize in a short phrase the details or facts the verses contribute toward the paragraph's amplification of the basic topic of the chapter or passage under study. Sometimes you will want to combine verses, but the general idea is first to see how *each* verse relates to the paragraph and the chapter (and the book).

Repeat this step for each paragraph in the chapter or passage. Write the main thought of each paragraph on a ladder rung and the subpoints in the space beneath. Put the verse numbers after each entry.

Step 4. How many rungs on the ladder did you use? The chart has a place for four, but they can vary between two and five. It will often divide into three, but don't think that an outline must have three points. If it has more than five, you should read and compare your main divisions again, because there probably are some that should be combined.

Sometimes there are some introductory verses, especially at the beginning of a book. These can be placed above the top rung on the chart. For example, "From Paul to the church at Corinth (vv. 1-2)."

PURPOSE OF THE LADDER BIBLE STUDY

There are three things we are trying to accomplish in this study: (1) identify the basic topic of the passage; (2) trace the development of the topic and reproduce it in a structural form; and (3) avoid using verses "out of context." You will not want to actually use a ladder diagram very many times, but you will want to think "ladder" and have the structure clearly in mind.

SUGGESTED STUDIES

Daily schedule

Sunday—2 Thessalonians 1
Monday—2 Thessalonians 2
Tuesday—2 Thessalonians 3
Wednesday—Philippians 1
Thursday—Philippians 2
Friday—Philippians 3
Saturday—Philippians 4

Weekly schedule

1 Timothy 6

Each day write out a personal application from the material you are studying.

SUGGESTIONS FOR THE TEACHER

If you can bring a little three foot step ladder to class, it will be very helpful to refer to during your Bible study. Even more helpful would be a small ladder of about the same height. To make one will require only a 1x2 inch beam, ten feet long. No great carpentry skill is required to build it.

Many people are going to need to be encouraged and assisted before they are convinced that they can learn to outline. Since some chapters are difficult to outline, select the easier ones to practice on first.

Students need to be convinced that they can outline, and they need to be convinced that it is an important skill that will make them better Bible students. Many pastors say that outlining a passage is one of the first steps in preparing an expository message. It not only aids the understanding but gives a more accurate interpretation of the Scriptures.

Don't be too quick to correct. A chapter can be outlined in several ways. Help the student test his outline. How does each main division relate to the topic of the chapter? Does it need to be reworded? Sometimes a division is all right, but it is not worded so as to show or emphasize its relationship to the chapter topic. It is not always easy to express in words what the mind is able to discern. Next, check the subpoints and their relationship to the chapter topic.

One problem that students often encounter is that they break a chapter down into too many pieces. They have too many fragments which, considered separately, cannot be related to the chapter topic. Writers often include parenthetical material, or develop several themes at one time. When this happens, you combine the verse or verses with the one before it that relates to the topic under discussion. In this way you account for all the verses in the chapter, but your subpoint only states how the portion is related to the main topic and does not try to describe all that the portion says. The important thing is that they understand what their problem is: fragmentation. The solution is to use longer portions so they can see the relationships.

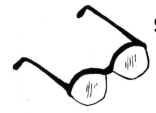

SPECS BIBLE STUDY

Bible Ref. _Eph. 6:10-24_

S ins to forsake-- *A lack of concern for others v.18, Insincerity in my love for Christ v.24.*

P romises to claim-- *God's armour will allow us to stand against the devil vs.11,13. Faith in the Lord will quench the attacks of the enemy v.16.*

E xamples to follow-- *Paul's desire to witness boldly v.19 Paul considered himself an ambassador v.20*

C ommands to obey-- *Be strong in the Lord v.10, put on the armour of God v.11, praying always v.18.*

S tumbling blocks or errors to avoid-- *Trying to engage the enemy in my own strength vs.10-12.*

N ew thoughts about God-- *God provides the power for victory. He gives peace and love v.23, He is greater than the enemy.*

P ersonal application of the Word to my life-- *I must claim by faith and use the power if I am to have victory in my life.*

64

10

Specs Bible Study

Many people find it necessary to wear glasses.* Your prayer should be that of the psalmist: "Open thou mine eyes, that I may behold wondrous things out of thy law" (Ps 119:18). You need to put on your spiritual "specs" to see yourself as God sees you, so the Holy Spirit can use the Bible to search your heart and point out your sins. "For the word of God is quick, and powerful, and sharper than any two-edged sword, piercing even to the dividing asunder of soul and spirit, and of the joints and marrow, and is a discerner of the thoughts and intents of the heart. Neither is there any creature that is not manifest in his sight: but all things are naked and opened unto the eyes of him with whom we have to do" (Heb 4:12-13). The Bible is also described as a glass or mirror in which you can see yourself (Ja 1:23-24).

You want the Holy Spirit to reveal Christ to you. From Genesis to Revelation, Christ is pictured in types, symbols, stories, and promises.

This is a devotional study; you are not studying the Bible now primarily to gain information but as a means through which God can speak to you.

Step 1. Do not hurry. Take a chapter or portion of a chapter and go over it slowly, asking yourself these questions. What—

Sin is there for me to forsake?

Promise is there for me to claim?

*This study is taken from the author's book *The Abundant Life* (Chicago: Moody, 1959), pp. 111-20. The book is a 12-lesson study guide.

*E*xample is there for me to follow?

*C*ommand is there for me to obey?

*S*tumbling block or error is there for me to avoid?

Make as short a note as possible; do not try to answer the questions in order, but keep them all in mind. In some portions you may not find an example to follow but there may be many promises to claim, or it may be the other way around.

When the Holy Spirit points out some sin, stop and confess it to God at once. Call it the same thing He does—gossiping, covetousness, unforgiveness, or lying. Then claim the forgiveness and cleansing of 1 John 1:9.

When you come to a *promise,* stop and claim it by faith and thank Him for it.

When you come to a *command,* stop and surrender to His will.

Step 2. Read through the passage again and ask yourself, "Has this passage taught me anything new about God or the person of Jesus Christ?"

Step 3. Now that the Holy Spirit has revealed some new things concerning God's will for your life, what are you going to do about it? Be definite in your personal application. Obedience means happiness (Jn 13:17). Disobedience or ignoring it is sin (Ja 4:17). God has thrown some light on your pathway, so write down a plan of action.

If you are studying in a group, ask each one if he will share the most meaningful thing from step 1 (SPECS). Some will have several things, but let each share one thing before you let any share a second idea. Do the same with thoughts about God and the personal applications.

PURPOSE OF THE SPECS BIBLE STUDY

This is a study that can be used day after day. It gives a workable plan for daily private devotions or "quiet time." Its purpose is to help you to develop your power of observation and to apply the Scripture to your life. These are skills that must be mastered under the ministry of the Holy Spirit.

Why not enroll in His school for the next week and do a SPECS each day?

SUGGESTED STUDIES

Daily Schedule

Sunday—Galatians 1
Monday—Galatians 2
Tuesday—Galatians 3
Wednesday—Galatians 4
Thursday—Galatians 5:1-15
Friday—Galatians 5:16-26
Saturday—Galatians 6

Weekly schedule

2 Timothy 1

Each day write out a personal application from the material you are studying.

SUGGESTIONS FOR THE TEACHER

A large percentage of people today wear eye glasses. Many are required by law to wear them when they drive an automobile. Ask all who wear glasses to remove them and then ask them to read an unfamiliar passage of Scripture such as Lamentations 3:19. Many will have great difficulty and others will not even be able to find the reference. Use this to illustrate the importance of having an open heart and being responsive to the Holy Spirit's ministry.

This study allows a big variety of responses. It is also one that can be utilized alone. Challenge them to use this as the basis of their morning devotions or "quiet time" for the following week. Use the daily schedule in the textbook. After the first week you can challenge them to finish the month. It will be a lot easier to get students to try a week, at first, rather than a month, of morning devotions.

 **BIBLE STUDY**

BIBLE REF. *Eph. 2:1-10*

Application(s): *I must be faithful in the work He has prepared me for and not just rejoice in my salvation.*

Best or basic verse: *Eph. 2:8-9*

C *I like 2:7 also because of the wonderful future planned.*

ross references:

V.	Ref.	Summary of Cross reference
1	Gen. 2:17	Disobedience to God will bring death
2	II Cor. 4:4	Satan is the god of this world
3	John 3:36	Wrath of God is on the unbeliever
4	Rom. 5:8	God proved His love by giving Christ for us
5	Rom. 6:4	We are raised with Christ
6	Eph. 1:20	Christ is at the right hand of God
8	John 5:24	Believers have everlasting life
9	Titus 3:45	Not saved by works of righteousness
10	Titus 3:8	Christians are to maintain good works

Digested (summary or outline): *You were dead spiritually and lived a lustful life under Satan. But God has made us alive in Christ and has a wonderful plan for us. He saved us by a gift of grace through our faith and prepared us to do good works.*

11

ABC Bible Study

The ABC Bible-Study method combines several skills used in previous lessons. By using about ten verses at a time, you can work your way through a book and when you are done you will have your own, private, little commentary.

Step 1. Read through the passage and then do part D: *d*igest it. Use the same method that you used in the Bible-gram or in the Funnel Bible Study. Summarize the content in your own words, using one word for each four or five of the text. Or, outline the passage as you did in the Ladder Bible Study. It will be helpful if you give it a title; it should be descriptive of the content of the passage.

Step 2. Try to find a *c*ross-reference for each verse in the passage. Use the same method used in the File Bible Study. It can be a parallel of a word, topic, or general teaching, but it should add new meaning. You are allowing Scripture to comment upon and explain Scripture.

Step 3. What do you personally think is the *b*est or basic verse? Why do you think it is? Some verses stand as the foundation upon which the rest of the passage builds. At other times the passage may lead to a certain conclusion. If you are studying with a group, be ready to tell why you picked this verse.

Step 4. Make a personal *a*pplication from this passage to your life. You may want to make several. When you have finished, you have said your ABC's in reverse order, finishing with the application.

PURPOSE OF THE ABC BIBLE STUDY

This plan combines several skills. You are challenged to complete at least one New Testament book using this method. Students in a Sunday school class could be encouraged to study their lesson in this way. Most will have to be taught the various skills (summarizing, outlining, cross-referencing, and making applications). If this is not done, they will feel inadequate and frustrated. The ABC Bible Study serves as an intermediate step between individual skills and the analytical book method of Bible study that is presented later.

SUGGESTED STUDIES

Daily schedule

Sunday—1 Peter 1:1-5
Monday—1 Peter 1:6-12
Tuesday—1 Peter 1:13-17
Wednesday—1 Peter 1:18-25
Thursday—1 Peter 2:1-8
Friday—1 Peter 2:9-16
Saturday—1 Peter 2:17-25

Weekly schedule

2 Timothy 2:1-14
2 Timothy 2:15-26

Each day write out a personal application from the material you are studying.

SUGGESTIONS FOR THE TEACHER

Bring a Scrabble game to class and give each student ten letters. At a signal, give them two minutes to use as many of their letters as they can in spelling one word. When they are finished, remind them that it is one thing to be able to recognize letters, but a different skill is required in order to be able to combine them into meaningful words.

In the same way, it is easier to do individual Bible study skills than it is to combine them into the meaningful Bible study of a passage. The ABC Bible study carries the student closer to the analytical book study method. It records the results of your study in a form that will have long-term benefits. Some students have used this method to study both large and small Bible books. One student spent a semester going through the book of Matthew paragraph by paragraph using the ABC method.

This method cannot be completed in a normal class hour. It is suggested that you start in class, doing step 1 and part of step 2, and let them bring it back to the next class meeting to share with one another. It takes time, but it is very rewarding and gives great personal satisfaction.

MICRO WORD STUDY

ENGLISH WORD _Temple_

REF. _I Cor. 6:19_

Meaning _Dwelling place, inner sanctuary_

Irregular translations _temple (45 times)_
shrine (1 time)

Context _an exhortation to live sexually pure_
lives.

Related words _Hebrew: Bayith, Hekal_
Greek: Hieron (usually refers to the temple as a whole)
Oikos (usually translated house) Naos (used to describe
the inner sanctuary of the temple where God dwells.

Original Hebrew or Greek _Naos_

PARAPHRASE THE VERSE: _" . . . your body is the sanctuary where_
the Holy Spirit dwells in you . . . " (I Cor. 6:19).

12

Micro Word Studies

The study of the words of Scripture is one of the most rewarding ways to study the Bible. It takes time and effort and requires some study tools, but it sheds light upon the message of the Word in ways that other methods cannot. Micro word studies, after the initial introductory lesson, should be completed at home and the results shared in classes. Most class periods are too brief to finish one in class.

Step 1. List the English word and the reference at the top of the page. Most study tools that we will be using are based upon the King James Version. Because several different Greek or Hebrew words may be translated by one English word (or one Greek or Hebrew word may be translated by several English words), it is necessary to cite the reference, so there will not be a misunderstanding as to what word is being studied.

Step 2. You will start at the bottom under section O and work your way up the page. First look up the word in *Young's Analytical Concordance to the Bible* (Grand Rapids: Eerdmans) and find what the original word is in either Hebrew (if it is in the Old Testament) or Greek (if it is in the New Testament). Consider the English word "sword." There are five Hebrew words translated by this one English word. All the references for any one word in the original are grouped together. If you want to find what Hebrew word is translated "sword" in Isaiah 2:4, you will find it in the second group (p. 950, column 3). This is the most common Old Testament word for sword. The listing starts in column one: "2. A sword, destroying weapon, חֶרֶב Chereb." The first thing that is given is a short literal meaning of the word. This is helpful, but it is a limited definition. Next is the Hebrew word spelled in Hebrew letters (the New Testament words are spelled in Greek letters). Following this, the Hebrew (or Greek) word is transliterated into English letters. Transliteration is the changing of the letters from one language into the letters of another. In contrast, translation is the changing of a word or expression from one language to the word(s) of another in an attempt to communicate the meaning. "Chereb" is the transliteration into English letters, and "sword" is the translation of this word into English. Enter the transliteration, chereb, on the line for O, Original language, along with the literal meaning, "A sword, destroying weapon." If your study tools tell you anything about the root the word comes from (or words, for it may be a compound), list this also in this section.

Step 3. List the other six related words that are translated "sword," and their literal meanings, under R, Related words. If you have the *An Expository Dictionary of New Testament Words* by W. E. Vine, you can improve upon the short definition that Young gives of each of these synonyms. Vine's book is a valuable study tool for Greek words. For Hebrew words, a valuable study tool is *Synonyms of the Old Testament* by R. B. Girdlestone. He does not cover as many Old Testament words as Vine does in the New Testament, but the book is good. He often relates the equivalent Greek word to the Hebrew.

Some words have opposites, such as "good and evil" or "hate and love." This type of word can best be understood when it is contrasted with its opposite or antonym. The antonym can also be listed in this section.

It is usually very helpful to ask yourself the questions, "Why was this distinct word chosen for this verse? What thought does it convey that others would not?"

Step 4. Look in the verse, paragraph, and chapter to determine the context in which the word is used. What is the subject under discussion? For example, in Hebrews 4:12 the word "sword" is used symbolically to describe the Word of God. It is not used to speak of a metal sword. But in Matthew 26:51 it is speaking of a real sword. The context can usually be stated in a short sentence. Enter this under C for Context.

Step 5. It is hard to find exact equivalents for words in another language. Because of history, culture, or other factors, words will differ from language to language. So, there will be occasions when a Hebrew (or Greek) word will be translated by several different English words. In the back of Young's concordance are two index lexicons: the first in Hebrew and the second in Greek. By looking up the transliterated spelling of the Hebrew word, "chereb," (p. 12, column 3), we find that it was translated: axe 1, dagger 1, knife 5, mattock 1, sword 402, and tool 1. List these under I for Irregular translations.

The most common translation is "sword," but this does not mean necessarily that every translation of it should be "sword." If you look up the word "axe" in the front of the concordance you will see that as it is used in Ezekiel 26:9, it could be either "axe" or "sword." Seeing all the English words that the translators have used to translate a word will give you a better understanding of the meaning. Of course, you should give the most emphasis to the English word that is used most to translate the Hebrew or Greek word.

Step 6. From your study write a distinctive definition of the meaning of this word. It should include the things that make it different from its synonyms. Don't make it too long. Enter this under M for Meaning. Try substituting your definition in some of the verses where the word is used. Using the reference listed on the top of your study, write out the verse (in the space provided at the bottom of this study). Substitute your definition in the verse. Does it help expand the meaning for you? It should. This approach is similar to the style of *The Amplified Bible*.

ADDITIONAL STUDY

As you study a word as it is used in a verse, you will note that it will change slightly according to how it is used: as a subject, object of the verb, adjective, or adverb. Verbs have several tenses, and words also may vary as to gender, number, or mood. Grammar and syntax are important. It helps to understand not only what the word means but also its exact form and use in the sentence. Unless you have had some study in the original languages, you will be dependent upon the commentaries for help in this area. They will often point out these distinctives and their significance. Good translations will often reflect some of these details also.

No word study is really complete unless you have studied a word in all its uses in the Bible. (On common words this is not practical or advisable.) This may take the form of a topical study. If the word is used many times, you may need to select a limited number of references or use only those from a book of the Bible.

A more limited study of some of the key words in a verse or paragraph is often helpful. For example, do the words "believeth" and "believeth not" in John 3:36 come from the same word in Greek? Is this word ever translated by another English word? What other reference gives a good example of the use of this word? You will often want to answer questions of this kind on your detailed paragraph studies (a step in the analytical study of a book). Complete chapter 17 on the use of the concordance outside of class.

PURPOSE OF MICRO WORD STUDIES

Word studies help you know *what the text says* and *what it means.* Many of the possibilities for the study of words are beyond the beginning student, but this should not be the basis for discouragement. Rather, it should be a challenge into a continued study of the Bible. Scholars after a lifetime of study admit that they have not exhausted the riches of God's Word.

SUGGESTED STUDIES

Daily schedule	*Weekly schedule*
Sunday—Redeemed (1 Pe 1:18)	Perfect (2 Ti 3:17)

Monday—Life (Jn 10:10; cf. v. 17)
Tuesday—World (1 Jn 2:15; cf. Mt 28:20)
Wednesday—Another (Gal 1:6-7)
Thursday—Repent (Mt 3:1-2)
Friday—Sanctification (1 Pe 1:2)
Saturday—Chasten (Heb 12:6)

Extra work

Reconciliation	Names of God
Temple	Sin
Prove	Peace
Fellowship	Minister
Prayer	Disciple
Man	

Each day write out a personal application from the word you are studying.

SUGGESTIONS FOR THE TEACHER

If you can find a real or toy microscope, it will make an ideal prop to bring to class. If not, use a reading or magnifying glass. Perhaps in an encyclopedia you can find a picture of some common object that is greatly enlarged and consequently shows details or colors that cannot be seen by the unaided eye. This illustrates that we can see an object but we really do not see it. In the same way we read words, but sometimes we do not really understand or appreciate what they mean.

This study takes a lot of effort. Many will not want to pay the price. It may be best that this be primarily a demonstration that the teacher presents. It will serve as a useful introduction on the use of the concordance. After this lesson, suggest that students complete the programmed instruction on the use of the concordance in chapter 17. To do it, they must be sold on two things: (1) that they can learn to do word studies and (2) that word studies are worth the effort.

A word of warning is in order. Be careful *not* to communicate to the student the idea that he cannot trust his understanding of the Bible unless he knows Hebrew and Greek. *Do* communicate the idea that word studies will give him a richer understanding of the Word.

After arriving at a good definition or meaning of a word, give each member of the class a different reference in which the word is used and have them read the verse and substitute the definition in place of the word.

TOPICAL BIBLE STUDY

Collect

Compare
(CLASSIFY)

CHERRIES   **APPLES**   **POTATOES**   **PUMPKINS**   **BEANS**

Construct

I. VEGETABLES

    A. BEANS   (GRADUATED ACCORDING TO

    B. POTATOES   SIZE IN THIS CASE)

    C. PUMPKINS

II. FRUIT

    A. CHERRIES

    B. APPLES

13

Topical Bible Studies and Biographical Studies

When studying a chapter or a book, you will sometimes realize that some topic is very prominent and much of what is said pertains to it. Or you may have a special interest in a certain topic or doctrine and you want to know what the Bible teaches about it. Because of the time involved, it is usually more practical to limit your study to a book. For example, "What does 1 Peter teach about suffering?" Or even limit your study to a chapter: "What does 1 Corinthians 15 teach about the resurrection?"

Step 1. Collect all the references in which the topic appears. This may be done in two ways: (1) Read through the passage and make notes. (2) Use your concordance. The first is best if time allows and if you are limiting your study to a book or a chapter. It will help you understand how the words are used, and you will not be as likely to use a verse out of context. But if you are doing a study on "fellowship" as found in the New Testament, you should use a concordance to help find all the passages, or you will have to read through the entire New Testament just to collect all of your material.

List each reference that refers to the topic under study and then summarize in a short phrase what the verse teaches or says about the topic.

Your study may be of a single word such as "love," or it may be on a topic such as "the testings of a Christian." In this case you would consider several words: "temptation," "trial," "persecution," "suffering," and related words. It will be easier to start with one word until you learn the method.

Using the word "hope," what does the book of Romans say about it? It should be noted that the Greek word translated hope means "confident expectation." In English we sometimes use it to mean "wish," as in "I hope it doesn't rain." This is not the meaning in Greek. Romans has the following twelve passages that deal with hope:

4:18—Abraham, humanly speaking, had no hope.
4:18—Abraham's hope was in the promise of God.
5:2 —Christians rejoice in the hope of the glory of God.
5:4 —Tribulation brings forth hope.
5:5 —Hope will not disappoint because of the Holy Spirit's ministry.
8:20—Present bad conditions will give way to the hope of a glorious liberty of the children of God.
8:24—We are saved by trusting in hope.
8:24—Hope that is seen is not hope.
8:25—Hope is something that you look forward to.
12:12—Christians should rejoice in hope.
15:4 —The Scriptures were given that we might have hope.
15:13—God is the God of hope.

Step 2. Compare or classify all the material. Ask yourself, "How can they be grouped or categorized?" Suppose a windstorm damaged a fruit and vegetable stand and mixed up all the merchandise and you were going to help set it back up. There are several approaches: collect or pick up all the produce, separate the fruit and the vegetables, separate the vegetables that grow above the ground from those that grow below the ground, separate the beans from the tomatoes, and separate the tomatoes according to varieties. It will depend upon your purpose as to how you classify your material. In this step you must decide upon your main categories or divisions.

82

In the study of "hope" in Romans, these classifications could be given:
1. The meaning of hope
2. The Christian's attitude toward hope
3. The source of hope

Having decided upon the classification, decide what references should go with each. The meaning of hope: 8:20; 8:24; and 8:25. The Christian's attitude toward hope: 8:24; 4:18; 12:12; 5:4; and 5:2. The source of hope: 15:4; 5:5; and 15:13. In this step, the classifications and the references within the classifications are not necessarily in order.

Step 3. Construct or organize the material. The parts now need to be put in a logical order. You use the same outlining skill studied in the Ladder Bible Study in chapter 9. First, consider the main divisions, "What order should they be in?" In the study of "hope," the following order is suggested:

    I. The meaning of hope for the Christian
   II. The source of hope for the Christian
  III. The proper attitude toward hope by the Christian

Notice that the titles have been changed a little. You will usually continue to change and work with your divisions and subpoints as you go along.

Having decided upon the order of the main divisions, you next put the material in each section in a logical order. You will also continue to work on your verse summaries so that they will relate to the main division that they are under.

    I. What is the meaning of hope for the Christian?
       A. Hope that is seen is not hope (8:24).
       B. Hope is something that you look forward to (8:25).
       C. Example: Bad conditions of the world will give way to a glorious liberty—the Christian's hope (8:20).
   II. What is the source of hope for the Christian?
       A. Hope comes from God, the God of hope (15:13).

B. Hope comes from the Scriptures given by God (15:4).

C. Hope will not disappoint because of the Holy Spirit's ministry (5:5).

III. What is the proper attitude toward hope by the Christian?

A. Hope should not rest in human ability (4:18).

B. Hope should rest in the promise of God (4:18). Abraham is the example.

C. Christians are saved by trusting in the hope promised by God (8:24).

D. Christians should not be discouraged by tribulation because God uses it to develop their hope (5:3-4).

E. Christians should rejoice in hope, knowing that hope is related to the glory of God (12:12; 5:2).

It is usually better to use complete sentences rather than just words or phrases in an outline. A sentence outline is much easier to use when speaking, and if you want to use it again at some future date, it will be easier for you to remember the contents.

BIOGRAPHICAL STUDIES

The method used in biographical studies is the same as the one used in topical studies. Collect the material, compare or classify the material, and construct or organize the material. There are two alternatives in the last step; you can organize it chronologically or thematically. Consider the life of David. If it is organized chronologically, it could be like this:

I. David's life as a shepherd

II. David's life in service under Saul

III. David's life as a fugitive

IV. David's life as a king

If the study is organized thematically, it could be like this:

I. David's homelife

II. David's political life

III. David's spiritual life

PURPOSE OF THE TOPICAL AND BIOGRAPHICAL STUDIES

The topical method will help you understand a doctrine or topic by bringing all the "pieces" together systematically so you can visualize it as a whole.

A biographical study can be very useful in communicating spiritual-life truth. Christians can learn much from the victories and failures of the lives of Bible characters.

When you have completed your outline, you will have the framework to build into a devotional or lesson. Add an appropriate introduction that points out the relevance of the topic, illustrations to help explain the various points, applications to relate the material to the lives of the audience, and a summary with the appropriate invitation or exhortation to action. You will then have a biblically based message that can be used by the Lord in your life and the lives of your listeners.

SUGGESTED STUDIES

Daily schedule
Sunday—Love in 1 Corinthians 13
Monday—Fruit-bearing in John 15
Tuesday—Submission in 1 Peter

Weekly schedule
End-time conditions as described in 1 and 2 Timothy (especially 2 Timothy 3)

Wednesday—Joy in Philippians
Thursday—Resurrection in 1 Corinthians 15
Friday—Biographical study of Stephen in Acts 6-7
Saturday—Biographical study of David in 1 Samuel 16-17

Each day write out a personal application from the material you are studying.

SUGGESTIONS FOR THE TEACHER

The topical Bible study will give a student a sense of accomplishment that is very rewarding. It brings order and understanding to a topic that previously was only a collection of isolated and sometimes apparently contradictory facts. It will give a skill that can be used effectively to minister to others by having well organized devotionals or talks (if you say, "sermons," you will frighten many).

Use the fruit and vegetable visual to explain the thought process of the steps in the topical method but use the ladder visual (chap. 9) to demonstrate the mechanical process of preparing the outline. First write the topic at the base of the ladder. After step 1, *collecting* all your material, and step 2, *comparing* or classifying the material, do step 3, *constructing* an outline, on the ladder. Put the main points or classifications on the rungs and then arrange the material in a logical order under each rung.

This method needs to be used several times in topical studies and biographical studies. Practice is important. The topical method is one of the methods studied in this book that has a permanent value, in contrast to some that are used just to teach a skill.

Chapter 16 presents a simple method of preparation for a devotional. A topical study can be used quite effectively as a devotional. Try to find places where your students can share their devotionals outside of the class, for example, Sunday school opening exercises, men's or women's groups, youth clubs, and rest homes.

ANALYTICAL CHART

BIBLE BOOK *Luke*

	MAIN DIVISIONS	Ch.	CHAPTER TITLES (OR SECTIONS)
THEME: The Son of Man, the heir of David, comes according to promise, presents Himself as Messiah, is rejected and crucified, rises from the dead and ascends to heaven.	The Son of Man's early life	1.	The birth of Jesus, heir of David, is *foretold*
		2.	Jesus' birth and childhood is recorded
		3.	Jesus is baptized and geneology is given
	The Son of Man, ministers in Galilee	4.	Jesus is tempted and ministers in Galilee
		5.	Jesus declares His deity
		6.	Jesus gives the sermon on the mount
		7.	Jesus raises the widows son from the dead
		8.	Jesus' ministry around the Sea of Galilee
		9.	Jesus' rejection is reported and death is foretold
	The Son of Man ministers in Judea	10.	Jesus sends out the seventy
		11.	Jesus teaches about true spirituality
		12.	Jesus teaches about hypocrisy and faithfulness
		13.	Jesus declares the necessity of repentance
	The Son of Man ministers in Perea	14.	Jesus teaches on discipleship
		15.	Jesus tells of the joy
		16.	Jesus teaches about life after death
		17.	Jesus tells of His second coming
		18.	Jesus tells of the rewards of following Him
		19.	Jesus travels to Jerusalem
	The Son of Man's Death and Resurrection	20.	Jesus is challenged by His enemies
		21.	Jesus foretells Jerusalem's fall
		22.	Jesus' last supper and arrest
		23.	Jesus is tried, crucified, and buried
		24.	Jesus appears to His followers

14

Charting a Bible Book

In studying a book of the Bible, it is necessary first to get an overview of the entire book. It really helps if one can see and understand the basic structure. One of the best ways to do this is by preparing an analytical chart. If it is a long book, the chart is prepared by using the chapter divisions; but if it is a short book, it is better to break the book down into paragraphs. Some translations are broken down into paragraphs. The New American Standard Bible uses the standard verse format but uses a bold type verse number to indicate the start of a new paragraph.

Step 1. Read through the book section by section (chapter by chapter, or paragraph by paragraph) and analyze the content as to subject matter. Give each section a title or short sentence that describes the content. This requires the same skill as used in the Funnel Bible Study. In it you took two steps: (1) you summarized the passage, using about one word for each four in the text, and (2) then you summarized the summary. Another approach is to ask yourself, "What is the basic topic of this section?" It might be "discipleship." Then ask yourself, "What is it saying about discipleship?" Your answer might be, "It costs to be a disciple."

Don't make the title too general or too short. It should be distinctive from other titles and complete enough so that next year, if you should read it, it will bring to mind what the section is about.

You will probably be dissatisfied with some of your titles, but you should be encouraged to keep working and changing them as you study in the book. As you search for the main divisions and subdivisions, you will want to rephrase some of them to show the relationship between the sections. Later, as you do detailed study in each chapter, you may find that you were not giving the proper emphasis in your title. But don't wait for perfection. It is important in this step to assign a title to it. Consider it "good until further notice."

At times you may want to make some section changes. You might want to combine several small paragraphs or divide a large one, which should be done because of subject content. Chapter and paragraph divisions are not part of the inspired text, and they have not always been divided at the best place. It will usually be best to avoid doing very much of this on the first version of your chart. Instead, do this in your revisions.

Step 2. Find and title your main divisions. By examining the title of each of the sections (paragraphs or chapters) and comparing it to the others around it, the structure can be discerned. Ask, "What do these paragraphs have in common?"

The same question can be used to test subdivisions within the main divisions.

The main divisions will usually come in the following places:

1. Between chapters (but sometimes in the chapter)
2. changes in time
3. changes in characters
4. changes in subject matter or topics
5. changes in geographical locations

Some prefer to enter their main divisions vertically on the chart. One of the advantages of an analytical chart is that several different types of main divisions can be entered on one chart. The book of Acts illustrates this. If divided by main characters, it could be: Ministry of Peter, chapters 1-12; and the Ministry of Paul, chapters 13-28. If divided by geography, it could be: Witness to Jerusalem, chapters 1-7; Witness to Judea and Samaria, chapters 8-12; and Witness to the Uttermost Part, chapters 13-28. The last section could be subdivided into the three missionary journeys of Paul and his imprisonment.

Step 3. Find the main theme of the book by comparing all the main divisions. What do they have in common? All together, what are they saying? You are summarizing the summaries of the summaries. State in one sentence the message of the book. This can be entered vertically along the left side of the main divisions, or some prefer placing it at the bottom of the chart.

After a detailed study of the book, you will probably want to revise the way you state your theme, but it is important to have at least a tentative idea before you begin a detailed study. When you have finished a detailed study of a Bible book, you should be able to take your revised statement of the theme and, starting with it, give a summary of the book, showing how the theme is developed section by section in the book.

PURPOSE OF THE ANALYTICAL CHART

Preparing a chart will give you a survey of the book's content. It also will help you discover the book's structure and serve as an intermediate step in outlining a book. If you will chart the large individual chapters, it will give additional practice in presenting the content of a paragraph in capsule form. Finally, it will help you see the book's theme or basic message and how it is developed.

SUGGESTED ANALYTICAL CHART STUDIES

Daily schedule	*Weekly schedule*
Sunday—1 Timothy	Analytical chart of
Monday—2 Timothy	2 Timothy 4, using
Tuesday—Mark 1-3	the following divisions:
Wednesday—Mark 4-6	4:1-2
Thursday—Mark 7-9	4:3-5

Friday—Mark 10-12   4:6-8
Saturday—Mark 13-16   4:9-13
                           4:14-18
                           4:19-22

Each day write out a personal application from the material you are studying.

SUGGESTIONS FOR THE TEACHER

An analytical chart will demonstrate its value repeatedly, but do not place too much emphasis on perfection. The chart can be compared to a captain's logbook. It is a record of experiences and observations as one journeys through a Bible book. Often a section will not be clearly understood until it is reviewed in the light of the whole journey or studied in detail.

It is important that each section (paragraph or chapter) be given a title as it is read, but the student is to be encouraged to put a "good until further notice" tag on it. Later he will be asked to rework his chart to describe more accurately the contents of the book.

Get a package of blank shipping labels (the kind you attach with a string), print "good until further notice" on them, and pass out one to each member of the class. This will do wonders in providing a non-threatening atmosphere.

In step two, if finding main divisions is difficult, select ahead of time two or three different main outlines from reference books in your library. Then if the students need help, ask them which outline seems the most logical. Or ask, "Can you take this outline and improve the divisions: either the verse divisions or the way they are stated?"

Learning to make a good analytical chart takes practice. Remember that it has three uses: (1) as a method for making a preliminary survey of a book, (2) as a way of finding the structure of a book, and (3) as an instrument to show a synthetic overview of a book after an analytical study of the book has been completed.

Verse	Paragraph Title	

Paul starts back to Jerusalem

Verse	
1.	<u>Departed</u> - God had revealed that His work in the area was done (Acts 19:21) (G.C.M. 466)
3.	There is a time to stand and a time to avoid trouble
6.	Luke joins the group
6.	<u>Days of unleavened bread</u> - a feast of Israel following the passover (Lev. 23:6-8)
7.	<u>Break bread</u> - Acts 2:42 practiced from the beginning I Cor. 11:26 "For as <u>often</u> as ye eat this bread... show the Lord's death..."
7.	<u>First day of the week</u> - James M. Gray says this is evidence that Sunday had replaced the Sabbath for Christian assemblies p. 469.
9.	<u>Dead</u> - was he dead or appeared to be dead?
10.	"Stop being alarmed, his life is still in him" (W.T.)
13.	Paul walked 20 miles, evidently alone, Troas to Assos. G.C.M. says he shows a rest and a restlessness - Rest in the Lord. "To me to live is Christ" Phil. 1:21 - Restlessness, a desire to push on, to see Rome and unevangelized places (Rom. 15:20,24).
16.	<u>Pentecost</u> came 49 days after passover, see v. 6
20.	<u>The Church of God which He purchased with His own blood</u> The deity of Christ is here asserted (J.M.G. 469)
21.	Notice the relation of repentance and faith.
22.	"I am impelled by the spirit to do so" (W.T.)
23.	Not a single impression.

15

Analytical Study of a Bible Book

In an analytical study of a Bible book, you use all the skills that you have been acquiring in the previous methods. It is something that will take time and effort, but it is very rewarding. It will allow you to master a book in a way that nothing else will do.

FOUR STEPS IN THE ANALYTICAL STUDY OF A BIBLE BOOK

1. Make a brief survey of the historical period and of the background of the book.
2. Read the book and make an analytical chart.
3. Make a detailed study of the book by sections: take notes on the text; make outlines, summaries, paraphrases, charts, and topical studies according to the material.
4. Make a synthetic study of the book.

Step 1. Using your reference books, such as *Unger's Bible Dictionary,* a Bible handbook or commentary, make a survey of the historical background of this period. Locate it in God's plan of the ages. Ask youself, "What historical and geographical data affect the understanding of this book? Who wrote it? Who are the recipients of this book? When was it written? If it is a historical book, what period of history does it cover? Who are the important characters in this book? What is the theme? What is the purpose behind this theme or message? What is a suggested outline (main divisions only) for this book?"

The Bible, and not the works of men. is your final authority. But you can share in the fruit of the study of great men of God. It can save you much time and effort if you learn to use reference books properly. Life is too short for you to study out everything for yourself. When you study the Bible, you should check out this survey information against what the text says. Put a mental tag on it: "Good until further notice." You may discover a way to outline the book that is better than the outline in the reference book or a different theme or purpose.

Step 2. Prepare an analytical chart of the book. This will give you a preliminary survey of the book itself and help you see the book's basic structure. Follow the instructions given in the chapter on analytical charts.

Step 3. Do detailed study of the book by paragraphs (or chapters). You will be using several skills learned from previous methods. You will make notes by verses concerning the following from your commentaries, concordances, Greek and Hebrew texts, translations, dictionaries, and other study aids, plus your own personal study and observations:

1. meaning of words and facts of grammar
2. cross-references
3. cultural, historical, or geographical data
4. identification of figures of speech
5. good translations or paraphrases of verses
6. interpretations

You want to record and preserve the fruit of your study. Using the method suggested, you can add to it in future years. It is poor stewardship to spend time in study and not have a way to save the results of your study. Start a new page for each section (paragraph or chapter). Do not write on the back now, but save it so you will have room several years from now when you are again studying this book. Make notes only on what is important. A good rule to go by is to ask yourself, "If I read this text a year from now, will I remember this fact?" If not, write it down. If you can answer, "Yes, I'll remember it," don't write it down, for it only fills up space and requires unnecessary work. It is not necessary to bring together all your thoughts and comments on one verse. You would do this only if you were writing your own commentary. This is a study sheet and you will normally make notes from one reference book at a time and only on the verses that the reference books help you on. Often, you will want to document the note. For example, you might record "Unger, p. 87" or "U 87." The basic purpose of this step is to help you understand exactly what the section of Scripture is saying.

When working in a chapter, there will be additional steps of in-depth study that you should make. It should include at least one of the following after you have completed your detailed paragraph study:

1. Make a detailed outline of the chapter.
2. Paraphrase the chapter verse by verse and try to capture the full meaning of the text in your own words.
3. Summarize the chapter or a doctrine or argument in the chapter.
4. Compare or contrast this chapter with other passages, or subjects or incidents in this chapter with one another. Sometimes charts are helpful.
5. Make a topical study of a doctrine in the book (or a chapter), or trace the development of a topic or theme through the book.
6. Make a biographical study of a character in the book.

When you have completed your detailed study, review the chapter (or paragraph) title that you had when you made your analytical chart. If it still accurately describes the content of this section of Scripture, enter it at the top of the page. If not, change it so that it more accurately records your present understanding of the chapter.

This step is not complete unless you make some type of application to your life and ministry. Whether on a formal or informal basis, it should have a practical purpose. Perhaps the best way is to keep a separate devotional application page.

Step 4. Develop a synthetic view of the book. You have made a preliminary survey of the background of the book, surveyed the contents by making an analytical chart, studied the book in detail, and now you want to put all the parts back together so they can be seen as a whole, a complex whole. This is what is meant by a synthetic view: see the book as a whole, yet be aware of the parts and how they all fit together. Your statement of the theme of a book should reflect your synthetic view of the book.

This step can be expressed in several ways. The most practical is to start by stating the theme of the book and showing chapter by chapter (or main division by main division) how the theme is developed in the book.

A revised and rephrased analytical chart also will reflect a synthetic view. But it will not be as easy for others to understand as it will be for you.

Your synthetic view can become a survey for a class or for someone else. It is useful to introduce the study of a Bible book, but it cannot truly be a synthetic view to them until they have studied the book in detail and have seen the "pieces" or details for themselves. When they have, they can see the book as a whole, yet be aware of the pieces and how they fit together.

Not many Christians invest the time necessary to gain a synthetic view of a book of the Bible. Why not be an exception?

A list of suggested Bible-study tools is given in chapter 18. The two following commentaries are available in inexpensive paperback editions and will be very useful for doing an analytical study of Colossians:

Harrison, Everett F. *Colossians: Christ All-Sufficient.* Chicago: Moody, 1971. This is a devotional commentary.

Wuest, Kenneth S. *Ephesians and Colossians.* Grand Rapids: Eerdmans, 1953. This is helpful for word studies and the Greek for the layman.

When you finish your analytical study of the book of Colossians, prepare a title page for it. You should be proud of it, for not one person in a thousand will have accomplished what you have. Your title page could look like this:

AN ANALYTICAL COMMENTARY
OF
COLOSSIANS
BY
SAM STUDYHARD

You also need to number your pages and prepare a contents page, such as this:

Contents

Future pages can be added to your notebook or file and put in their proper place by numbering 5a, 5b, 7a, 10a, et cetera. Using this method, it is not necessary to renumber all the pages. If necessary, you could insert twenty-six additional pages between any that you have in your original work. If you add more than this, you'd better retype it and get it published, because you will have written a book!

SUGGESTED ANALYTICAL BOOK STUDY

Colossians
Sunday—Background of historical period and Colossians
Monday—Analytical chart of Colossians

Tuesday—Detailed paragraph study of 1:1-17

Wednesday—Paraphrase 1:1-17 using the results of Tuesday's study

Thursday—Detailed paragraph study of 1:18-29

Friday—Summarize 1:18-29 (average one word for four)

Saturday—Detailed chapter study of chapter 2

Sunday—List all the ways we are identified with Christ in chapter 2

Monday—Detailed paragraph study of 3:1-13

Tuesday—Detailed paragraph study of 3:14-25

Wednesday—Outline 3:1—4:1

Thursday—Detailed chapter study of chapter 4

Friday—List all the prayer requests given in Colossians

Saturday—Do a topical study on the doctrine of Christ in Colossians

Sunday—Review and revise your analytical chart and then state the theme of the book and write a synthetic study

Extra assignment—Compare the doctrine of Christ as taught in Colossians with John 1 and Hebrews 1

Each day write out a personal application from the material you are studying.

SUGGESTIONS FOR THE TEACHER

This study is the climax of the methods presented in this book. All the various skills are brought together and used. In the detailed paragraph study, students will: (1) make observations, as they did in the Heart Check, SPECS, Weather Report, and SOAP; (2) find cross references as they did in the FILE; (3) compare translations as they did in the Panel and Clock; (4) do word studies as they did in the MICRO; and (5) write paragraph titles as they did in the SOAP, Funnel, and Analytical Chart.

On some occasion they will outline, as in the Ladder, summarize, as in the Biblegram and Funnel, make topical or biographical studies, and chart the chapters and the book.

Stress that they have already performed all of the study

skills which now are being used together. Therefore, they can do it.

Step 3, the detailed study of each paragraph, will vary from paragraph to paragraph. Usually a *detailed* paragraph study should be completed for each paragraph, plus at least one of the *additional* six methods of developing the paragraph (outline, paraphrase, summary, comparison or contrast, topical study, or biographical study). Topical studies should be made of the important themes or doctrines of the book. The subject should dictate the method chosen rather than simply picking an easy method. If skills are properly applied, upon completing the study of a book, a student will feel that he really understands the book. Not that he knows everything, but that he understands the basic message and can trace its development. He will also have completed his own personal commentary of the book, and when it is in such a form, he can add new thoughts to it as the years go by. Encourage the students to buy the paperback commentaries suggested in the text. Have available any of the other suggested Bible study tools that you can assemble. They need to become acquainted with them so they can understand their value.

HOW TO PREPARE A DEVOTIONAL

State your main point clearly.

Explain: restate, give more details, give opposite, illustrate.

Apply to life experiences.

16

How to Prepare a Devotional

Have you been asked to have a devotional for a class or some other occasion? Perhaps you don't know what is expected, or perhaps you don't know how to go about it. These opportunities should not be allowed to slip away but, rather, to be utilized for the Lord. But first let us get our definition clear: "What do we mean by devotional?"

Devotion is usually connected with the idea of worship or the life that is "devoted to God." In the minds of many, it would pertain to anything related to the spiritual life. On some occasions it might be thought of as an evangelistic message also, but this is the exception rather than the rule, for Christian devotion is connected with Christians, not non-Christians. (Of course, other religions have their devotional exercises also.) But for our purposes, one characteristic of a devotional would be that the subject matter is related to the spiritual life.

The word "devotional" is sometimes used to describe a short message. It might be used to open a Sunday school department session, a club meeting, convention session, or social affair. It may take five minutes in contrast to a sermon that lasts for thirty. Because of its brevity it will differ in structure. But if it is going to be effective, it must be structured and well planned. Think about some of the devotionals you have heard. If you were asked to evaluate them, what would be your criticisms?

103

"He didn't really have anything to say; just the same old clichés and platitudes." "He rambled or got off on a tangent and didn't seem to have any goal. Hard to understand how some parts were related." "He didn't know when to quit." "Can't see how this devotional relates to me." Do these comments strike a familiar chord?

HAVE ONE MAIN THOUGHT

If we could establish one basic rule it would be, "Have one main thought," This essential, or you won't know how to get started, you won't have a basis for organizing your thoughts, and you won't know when to quit. Remember, you have a limited amount of time; you can't cover very much. Besides, you don't want to have a "garage sale" of good ideas, or people will "browse around" and go home with nothing. Usually people try to cover too big a subject; this is a pitfall to avoid. You do not pick a general topic.

"The discipline of God" is too big a subject to cover in a devotional. It has many aspects: the relationship of discipline to salvation, the purpose of discipline, the kinds of discipline, and the results of discipline. All of these are too big. Let us take this thought as an example: God disciplines Christians because He loves them. If you can't say what you have to say in one good sentence, you need to work on it some more and probably limit what you have to say.

USE THREE BASIC STEPS

In any kind of communication you have one basic purpose: You want to transport your cargo of thought to your listener (reader or viewer). If he does not take it home with him, you have failed. One suggestion is for the body of your devotional to have the following three basic steps:

State Your Main Point Clearly

You may clearly understand what you are talking about, but remember that you have been studying and meditating on it, while your listener has not. So state your main point as clearly as possible. It will almost always be based on a verse or short passage of Scripture, and this would be the appropriate time to read or refer to it. For example, "God disciplines Christians because He loves them. Revelation 3:19 says, 'As many as I love, I rebuke and chasten.'"

Explain Your Main Point

Your main point should be able to stand alone, but you can reinforce its effectiveness by explaining it. The Hebrew writers of the Psalms used a method that is helpful. After making a statement, they sometimes would restate the same idea in a different way. For example, "Shew me thy ways, O LORD" and the next phrase which restates the idea, "Teach me thy paths" (Ps 25:4).

At other times in the second line they gave additional details: "Then will I teach transgressors thy ways;" and the second statement, "and sinners shall be converted unto thee" (Ps 51:13). See also Psalm 19:1.

Making a statement and then contrasting it with an opposite statement is another method used in the Psalms. Compare the positive and negative statements in Psalm 1.

Another way of explaining your main point is to use an illustration. This can be a short story, anecdote, personal experience, or even a joke if it is appropriate, but it must illustrate the main point. Avoid the pitfall of having such an interesting illustration that your audience misses the main point. It is supposed to explain the main point, not attract attention to itself or to you. Sometimes visual illustrations, such as a picture, a drawing, or an object of some kind, are very helpful.

We could illustrate how a human parent disciplines his child so that he doesn't play in the street and get injured. A pictorial illustration, such as a picture of a patient in a hospital or of an ambulance, might also be used. Extra details could be given, such as the meaning of the word "chasten." An opposite or contrasting statement, which explains that by discipline we do not mean an eternal penal judgment, could be made. The exact method and extent that you explain and illustrate will depend upon the subject matter. Often it is good to repeat the text of Scripture on which you are basing your devotional after this explanatory step.

APPLY YOUR MAIN POINT

If the truth of the devotional is not related to life, it becomes just an intellectual exercise. One pitfall that is often made is to assume that the listeners will automatically relate the devotional to their life experiences. But you need to apply it for them.

If it is because of God's love that He disciplines me, I shouldn't resent or rebel at that discipline. The next time I am aware that I am being disciplined, I should ask myself, "What is God trying to teach me? How can I profit spiritually from this experience?" When you have made your application, repeat your main thought: "God disciplines us because He loves us," and then quit.

The first letters in each of the basic steps used in preparing the body of your devotional collectively spell "SEA." If you are going to transport your cargo of thought to your listeners, you must take them across this SEA:

State your main point clearly.

Explain: restate, give extra details, give opposite thoughts, and then illustrate.

Apply the main thought to the life experiences of your listeners.

HOOK YOUR LISTENERS

The introduction of the devotional, while short, must attract or "hook" the interest of the listeners. Sometimes this can be done by using a question, startling statement, a short quotation, or a short anecdote. It should capture his attention and point to the relevance of what you are going to say. You should not tell a joke and then say, "Now I would like to share some serious thoughts with you." If the situation is proper for a joke, the right kind of joke could lead into or illustrate the significance of the devotional. Such a question as this might be used: "Why do Christians always seem to get caught when they break the law, and unsaved people seem to get away with everything?"

If you use a title, it can sometimes also help "hook" the attention of the listeners. After asking the above question, you might continue, "I would like to speak upon the subject, 'Why the good get caught and the bad go free.'" You can, if you prefer, give your title and then ask the question. It then would be easy to move on to your main thought: that it is God disciplining us because He loves us. Work on your opening statement until you practically have it memorized. Do the same for your closing. If you start well, have an orderly progression across the SEA, and then end when you get there, you will find you have successfully transported your cargo of thought, and your devotional will have had a ministry.

Now, here is a challenge. Will you ask the Lord to give you the opportunity to prepare and give a devotional?

SUGGESTIONS FOR THE TEACHER

This chapter can be used in class or out of class. If a person can learn to get up and start with a good introduction, without excuses, without jokes that have no connection with the devotional, and without rambling, he will be different from most who give devotionals.

If he can present his thought in an organized way, he will have made a second notable achievement. Most people have a bunch of good things they try to present.

If he can make a good application that applies to his audience and summarize his devotional with a good conclusion, and then quit, he will be a winner. Many people, once they get started, have a hard time finding a way to stop.

If you can communicate the importance of working out the introduction (have them write it out so they know what they are going to say), organizing the message (test it according to the SEA pattern), and working out the conclusion (write it out), you will have helped the students learn to successfully prepare a devotional.

Next, prayerfully help them find places to give the devotionals, and challenge them to do so.

17

Learning to Use an Analytical Concordance

The concordance is one of the most important tools used in Bible study. It is an alphabetical index of words found in the Bible, together with their context. The phrase and reference in which a word appears is listed. For example, the word "reed" is used in eleven places in the New Testament, and Matthew 27:30 lists this phrase: "took the reed, and smote him on the head."

Small concordances are printed in the back of many Bibles, but these are quite limited in use because they only list the more important words and references. Some concordances are for special translations, such as the one for *The Living Bible*. The three most popular concordances for English readers and prepared for the King James Version of the Bible are Young's, Strong's, and Cruden's. They are recommended in that order. Cruden's does not make any distinction between the different words in the original. Young's and Strong's both do, but it is my opinion that Young's is much more versatile. There is not a comparable analytical concordance available for any of the new translations. This chapter has been programmed to teach the use of Young's. It cannot be used with Strong's or Cruden's.

USES OF YOUNG'S ANALYTICAL CONCORDANCE

Upon completion of this chapter you should be able to use Young's concordance to help you study in the following ways:

1. to locate the reference for any verse even if you only remember part of the verse
2. to find all the references for any English word used in the Bible so you can find parallels of words, ideas, or topics
3. to tell what Greek or Hebrew word any English word is translated from. (Sometimes one English word is used to translate a dozen different Hebrew and Greek words.)
4. to find the way a word is spelled in the original
5. to give the transliterated spelling in English letters
6. to give a short literal meaning of the word
7. to find how many different English words are used to translate a Hebrew or Greek word. (Sometimes a dozen are used.)
8. to know what stem of the Hebrew verb is used: active or passive, simple, intensive, causitive, or reflexive (in other words, whether the subject is acting, being acted upon, or acting upon himself, and with what intensity the action is being performed.)

THIS CHAPTER IS DIFFERENT

In intrinsic programming, or a "scrambled text," you cannot read straight through the program. This chapter is set up like a program. You will be asked a question and then given a choice of answers. The *answer* you pick will have a section *number* next to it, which is the paragraph you should read next. If you understood the question and picked the correct answer, it will give you some new material and another question and send you on. If you had trouble with the answer, it will correct your answer or give you additional information, or send you back to pick a new answer. The principle is that it will give help when it is needed but will not force you to go over material that you know. Your journey through the chapter will be different from others. This is *not* an examination; it is an instructional method. By the time you finish the chapter you should be able to use the concordance. Because it is a scrambled text, you need to keep a record of your steps.

Enter them in order in the following chart and do not change them if you pick a wrong answer. The wrong answer will tell you where to go to find the right answer.

CONCORDANCE STUDY

YOUR RECORD OF STEPS:

1   52   54   58

(The first steps are filled in to help you understand how to record your work.)

No. 1 Read the "Preface" and "Hints and Helps to Bible Interpretation" in *Young's*. Where do they begin?
—They begin on page i.   section 50
—They begin on page iv.   section 52

No. 2 How did you get to this section? If you had followed instructions, you couldn't possibly be here. Do you want to have to stay after school? Seriously, you must go back to section 1 and follow instructions. This chapter will not make any sense if you try to just skim through it. It is scrambled.

No. 3 YOUR ANSWER: *Promotion.* You are correct. Now look this up in your concordance. On what page and column is it found in your concordance?
—page 443, column 2   section 12
—page 779, column 1   section 20

No. 4 YOUR ANSWER: *Matthew 19:28.* This verse uses the word "throne," but it is not the verse we are looking for. Go back to section No. 11 and pick another answer.

No. 5 YOUR ANSWER: *God.* You could find it this way. Let's try it; turn to it in your concordance. What do you find? Over twelve pages of references! You'll think you are read-

111

ing the whole Bible before you find it, because it is on the seventh page. Go back to section 9 and pick a better word.

No. 6 YOUR ANSWER: *Crown.* Guessed wrong, didn't you? Don't blame yourself. You have to try each possibility until you find the right one. Go back to section 25 and try again.

No. 7 YOUR ANSWER: *Page 879.* Correct. Now we have four other verses to give you practice. Do all four and then check your answers.
1. The Bible says that before the Messiah comes in judgment, Elijah must return. _____ (ref.)
2. Jesus said that if the weary would come unto Him, He would give them rest. _____ (ref.)
3. That the Lord will return and His feet will stand on the Mount of Olives. _____ (ref.)
4. In contrast to thinking about evil things, the Bible says we are to think on good things such as what is true and honest. _____ (ref.) It should be noted that all of the above are only paraphrases and are meant to approximate the way you would be able to remember a verse. Don't worry if you miss one. These are difficult problems. Check your answers in section 34.

No. 8 YOUR ANSWER: *Neither of these.* You are wrong. Go back to section 20 and pick another answer.

No. 9 YOUR ANSWER: *Pick the most uncommon word.* You are correct. Now which of the following words would you pick?
—promotion	section 3
—but	section 16
—God	section 5

No. 10 YOUR ANSWER: *Sceptre.* Correct. Now if you haven't just guessed without looking up the reference, the verse should be found at
| —Hebrews 1:8 | section 28 |
| —Genesis 49:10 | section 21 |

No. 11 YOUR ANSWER: *Psalm 75:6.* Correct. Actually you need verse 7 also. Quite often we misquote verses and when we try to look up the most uncommon word, it isn't in the concordance with a reference that refers to the verse we wanted. You have two alternatives: (1) look up a synonym of the word you couldn't find, or (2) use a different word that you remember is in the verse. The second way is usually best. It is difficult to give you practice, because I have to pick a verse we hope you have heard but don't remember the reference for. Let's consider a new verse that goes something like this: "The throne will not depart from Judah until Shiloh comes." Look up the word "throne." What is the reference of the above verse?

—Genesis 41:40	section 19
—Matthew 19:28	section 4
—neither of these or any that are listed	section 25
—my reference is_____	section 17

No. 12 YOUR ANSWER: *Page 443, column 2.* You are guessing. Look it up in your concordance and then check your answer against section 3.

No. 13 YOUR ANSWER: *Pick the most common word.* No, you are wrong. Read section 58 again and pick the correct answer.

No. 14 YOUR ANSWER: *Two Hebrew and one Greek.* No, there are three different words, but this is not the right combination. They are all Hebrew because they are all in the Old Testament. Go back to section 34.

No. 15 YOUR ANSWER: *Can't find it.* Look near the top of page 879, column 3. It is all by itself. This neglecting to look under *all* listings happens quite often. At other times, you will just miss it. It will be there but you won't see it. It happens to all of us. Go on to section 7.

No. 16 YOUR ANSWER: *But.* I said the most uncommon

word, not the shortest. Return to section 9 and pick the correct answer.

No. 17 YOUR ANSWER: *My reference is* _____. I don't know what you have found, but it doesn't say, "The throne will not depart from Judah until Shiloh comes." Remember, we are trying to find *this verse* and not just a verse that uses the word "throne." Go back to section 11 and pick the correct answer.

No. 18 YOUR ANSWER: *Six Hebrew words.* No, there are six references listed but not that many different Hebrew words. Look again and then go back to section 34 and pick the correct answer.

No. 19 YOUR ANSWER: *Genesis 41:40.* This is the first reference listed in the concordance for the word "throne," but it doesn't say, "The throne will not depart from Judah until Shiloh comes." Go back to section 11 and pick another answer.

No. 20 YOUR ANSWER: *Page 779, column 1.* Correct. Now, look up the references in your Bible and see if either of the two that are listed are correct.
—Psalm 75:6	section 11
—Proverbs 3:35	section 64
—neither of these	section 8

No. 21 YOUR ANSWER: *Genesis 49:10.* Correct. Instead of looking up synonyms for "throne," we could have chosen another word in the verse such as "Shiloh." Look this up. What page of the concordance will you find Genesis 49:10 listed under Shiloh?
—page 843	section 30
—page 879	section 7
—can't find it	section 15

No. 22 YOUR ANSWER: *(1) Temple, 3 Hebrew and 3 Greek; (2) Song, 8 Hebrew and 1 Greek; (3) Passover, 1 Hebrew and 1 Greek.* Is the word translated "wind" in Mark

4:37 the same as the one translated "wind" in John 3:8?

—Yes	section 39
—No	section 29

No. 23 YOUR ANSWER: *One Hebrew.* No, there are more than that. One English word is used to translate several words. Look again on page 339 and then go back to section 34.

No. 24 YOUR ANSWER: *Yes.* You are wrong. Did you guess? Go to section 37 and I'll give you a hint.

No. 25 YOUR ANSWER: *Neither of these or any that are listed.* Correct. The word "throne" is the wrong word. Section 11 tells you that there are two things you can do. Do you remember what they are? If not, review now. If "throne" isn't the exact word the verse uses, it might be one of the following words. Pick one and look it up in your concordance *before* you check your guess.

—crown	section 6
—sceptre	section 10

No. 26 YOUR ANSWER: *Five.* Correct. But these five words are *not* always translated "world." In order to be able to find if any Greek or Hebrew word is translated by more than one English word, you need to go the the Index-Lexicon to the Old Testament for Hebrew and Aramaic words (the Aramaic words are printed in italic or slanted capitals) and the Index-Lexicon to the New Testament for Greek words. The words are listed alphabetically by their transliterated spellings. Each of the lexicons is numbered separately. You may get then mixed if you don't put bookmarks at the start of each or make cellophane tape tabs. If you are able to tell the difference between Hebrew and Greek characters, this also will help you. Go back to the word "world" in your concordance and look at the eighth group of references listed, under the Greek word that has the transliterated spelling "gē." Look this up in the lexicon for the New Testament. How many words do you find listed under it?

—five   section 43
—seven   section 32
—I can't find it; I need help.   section 45

No. 27 YOUR ANSWER: *Age(s)–Ephesians 2:7; Colossians 1:26 (found on p. 21, center column); course–Ephesians 2:2 (p. 207, center column).* By doing this for all six words that are used to translate the word *aion,* you can find every place this word is used in the Bible. The other advantage in being able to tell what is the original word is that a literal translation often makes the meaning clearer. If Matthew 28:20, Romans 12:2, Ephesians 1:21, and Hebrews 6:5 are translated "age" (as Eph 2:7 and Col 1:26 are in the KJV), it makes the meaning much clearer. Look up each of these passages and instead of using "world" use "age" and notice the difference. Now look up the word "precious" and see how many Greek words are translated by this word. Check your answer in section 41.

No. 28 YOUR ANSWER: *Hebrews 1:8.* No! This uses the word "sceptre" but it is not the verse we want. Check the references in the concordance again, then go back to section 10 and pick the right answer.

No. 29 YOUR ANSWER: *No.* Correct, the first is *anemos* and the second is *pneuma.* One of the words translated "temple" means "inner sanctuary." Is this what Jesus cleansed in John 2:14-15? Check and then turn to section 36.

No. 30 YOUR ANSWER: *Page 843.* No, you are wrong. Either you guessed or you are still on the page where the word "Sceptre" is found, rather than where "Shiloh" is found. Look it up in the concordance then go back to section 21 and pick another answer.

No. 31 YOUR ANSWER: *Seven.* You missed by one; count again and then go back to section 41 and pick the right answer.

No. 32 YOUR ANSWER: *Seven.* This is correct if you

count every word. Following the word "country" is the number "2." This means that *gē* is twice translated "country." It is translated "earth" 188 times, but the translators one of these times gave a marginal translation of "land." That is what (M. land 1) means. When two or more words in the original are translated by one word or a phrase, it is preceded by a cross. That is what "earthly" means at the bottom of the list. These explanations are given at the beginning of each lexicon, and some are at the bottom of the page. Read them. Now look up in the lexicons each of the Hebrew and Greek words listed under "world" and count the different English words that they are translated by. Omit any marginal renderings or those preceded by a cross. When you have finished, turn to section 46 and check your answers. Don't cheat yourself; do the work.

No. 33 YOUR ANSWER: *Ten.* You weren't listening. I asked for only the Greek and you also gave me the Hebrew. Count them again and then go back to section 42.

No. 34 YOUR ANSWER: *(1) Malachi 4:5; (2) Matthew 11:28; (3) Zechariah 14:4; (4) Philippians 4:8.* The words from your English Bible (KJV) are listed alphabetically in your concordance, but they are grouped analytically. The references are grouped under each English word according to the original Hebrew or Greek word from which it is translated. Look up the word "dog." This is translated from one Hebrew and two Greek words (Hebrew will have Old Testament references, and Greek will have New Testament references). Under each of these subdivisions it will give three things: (1) a short literal translation, (2) the Hebrew or Greek spelling; and (3) a transliteration (spelling the Hebrew or Greek word with the English alphabet). The literal translation of No. 1 is "dog"; No. 2 is "little dog"; and No. 3 is "dog." The transliteration of No. 1 is *keleb;* No. 2 is *kunarion;* and No. 3 is *kuon.*

Now look up the word "feather." How many different Hebrew or Greek words are translated "feather"?

117

—one Hebrew word	section 23
—three Hebrew words	section 38
—six Hebrew words	section 18
—two Hebrew and one Greek word	section 14

No. 35 YOUR ANSWER: *Six.* Correct. Now, see if the word *timios* is translated by any words besides "precious." If it is, list them; then turn to section 44 to check your answers.

No. 36   YOUR ANSWER: *No, it is not the same.* It is the Greek word *hieron.* The inner sanctuary is the word *naos.* Is the word translated "babe" in Luke 2:16 the same as the word translated "child" in Luke 2:27?

—yes	section 24
—no	section 42
—I don't know how to tell;	
I need help	section 37

No. 37 YOUR ANSWER: *I need help.* This is the way you do it: Look up the word "babe" and see what the transliterated word is for Luke 2:16. Then look up the word "child" in Luke 2:27 and compare them. Now go back to section 36 and pick the correct answer.

No. 38 YOUR ANSWER: *Three Hebrew words.* Right, and you know they are all Hebrew, even though you can't read Hebrew, because they are all Old Testament references. How many different Hebrew and Greek words are translated by the following: (1) Temple, (2) song, and (3) Passover? When you have looked all of these up, turn to section 22.

No. 39 YOUR ANSWER: *Yes.* You are wrong. Mark 4:37 is under 2. *anemos;* John 3:8 is under 3. *pneuma.* Look again and return to section 22.

No. 40 YOUR ANSWER: *Jeremiah 31:20.* You fell into a trap. The literal meaning of the Hebrew word translated "dear" also means precious, but it is not *timios.* Go back and check your concordance; then return to section 44.

No. 41 YOUR ANSWER: *It should be three*. Now check all four listings (including the compounds) on page 769. How many times does "precious" appear in 1 and 2 Peter?
—six   section 35
—seven   section 31

No. 42 YOUR ANSWER: *No*. You are correct. The word "babe" is translated from *brephos,* and "child" is translated from *paidion.* The occasion in Luke 2:27 took place forty-one days after the birth of Jesus, and a different word is used for a child of this age. By using your concordance in this way you can make such distinctions. Sometimes our translations use one English word to translate ten or twenty different Hebrew and Greek words. This is not necessarily a fault of the translators because languages have many words that have no exact equivalents.

It is also true that as many as ten different English words may be used to translate one Hebrew or Greek word. Your concordance will help you know if any Hebrew or Greek word is translated by more than one English word.

Look up the word "world" and see how many Greek words are translated by this one English word.
—five   section 26
—ten   section 33
—eleven   section 59
—eighteen   section 49

No. 43 YOUR ANSWER: *Five*. Correct, but there are some extra words listed. Let's go to section 32 and talk about them.

No. 44 YOUR ANSWER: *It is also translated "dear" 1 time, "had in reputation" 1 time, "honourable" 1 time, and "precious" eleven times*. This is found in the New Testament lexicon on page 93. Find the reference for the place where *timios* is translated "dear."
—Jeremiah 31:20   section 40
—Ephesians 5:1   section 47
—Acts 20:24   section 48

No. 45 YOUR ANSWER: *I need help.* Turn to page 71, in the New Testament lexicon (not the Old), and look in column five about two inches from the bottom. Then turn back to section 26 and pick the correct answer.

No. 46 YOUR ANSWER: *erets,* 10; *chedel,* 1; *cheled,* 3; *olam,* 20; *tebel,* 3; *aion,* 6; *aionon* (evidently 1, not listed); *ge,* 5; *kosmos,* 2; *oikoumene,* 2. (If you missed these, did you look them up in the lexicon in the back?)

Now, how do you find where the references are where different English words have been used to translate these original words? By looking up the Greek or Hebrew word in the lexicon. For example, under the word *oikoumene* we found that fourteen times it was translated "world", but once it was translated "earth." Look up "earth" in the front of the concordance (pp. 280-83). Word list 9 in the third column of page 283 shows that *oikoumene* was translated "earth" in Luke 21:26. Now let's take a new problem. The word *aion* is translated "world" and five other words. Find the references where it is translated "age" and "course." After you have listed them, turn to section 27 and check your answers.

No. 47 YOUR ANSWER: *Ephesians 5:1.* Wrong, you are looking for the word *timios.* Check the concordance and then return to section 44.

No. 48 YOUR ANSWER: *Acts 20:24.* Correct. Read again paragraph one on page iv of the introduction "Prefatory note to the First Edition." Young numbers the different stems of the Hebrew verbs. We are putting this in a chart form:

Voice	Simple (Number) (Name)		Intensive (Number) (Name)		Causitive (Number) (Name)	
Active	1	Kal	3	Piel	5	Hiphil
Passive	2	Niphal	4	Pual	6	Hophal
Reflexive			7	Hithpael		

120

Any verb that does not have a number after it in the concordance is a *Kal,* or number 1. It is the normal way of using that verb in the active voice, and Young does not list it. Look up the word "covet" found in Deuteronomy 5:21. When you have found the number, turn to section 63.

No. 49 YOUR ANSWER: *Eighteen.* You made a mistake. You counted both Greek and Hebrew. Also, we want to lay some ground rules for these exercises, so turn to section 59 for additional instructions.

No. 50 YOUR ANSWER: *They begin on page one.* It might seem logical, but this is wrong. Look again and then return to section 1.

No. 51 YOUR ANSWER: *It should have been only Proverbs 21:26.* If you listed Acts 20:33, you need to stop and get a cup of coffee and wake up because you aren't thinking. The New Testament is written in Greek, and the verbs would not be Hebrew stems. The other two are from different words. What stems are they?
  —They are not verbs.   section 66
  —*Kal* or number 1   section 68
  —I need help.   section 53

No. 52 YOUR ANSWER: *Page iv.* Right! You had to count back from page ix to find out, but you did it. What concordance is this program designed for?
  —Cruden's   section 54
  —Strong's   section 60
  —Young's   section 58

No. 53 YOUR ANSWER: *I need help.* The answer is that they are *Kal,* or number 1. Review section 48 and then go on to section 68.

No. 54 YOUR ANSWER: *Cruden's.* I do believe that you have been sleeping in class. Go back to section 52 and pick the correct answer.

No. 55 YOUR ANSWER: *It should be like this:*

Isaiah 30:33	passive	6	it has been caused to be prepared
Psalm 23:5	active	1	thou preparest a table
Jeremiah 6:4	active	3	Strongly prepare ye war
Jeremiah 12:3	active	5	[cause] to prepare them
Psalm 59:4	reflexive	7	They . . . prepare themselves

Now it is time to review. If you want to find all the Hebrew and Greek words that are translated "prayer," you should:

—Look in the main concordance   section 62
—Look in the lexicons in the
    back   section 67

No. 56. YOUR ANSWER: *By looking up the Greek or Hebrew word in the main part of the concordance.* Wrong. Go back to section 62.

No. 57 YOUR ANSWERS: *(1) 5 Hebrew, 5 Greek; (2) Manner, means, or period of life; (3) animal life, breath; (4) zoe; (5) yes, heart, life, mind, soul, heartily; (6) No; (7) psuche; (8) Yes, (9) age, indefinite time, dispensation; (10) Yes, allow, approve, discern, examine, like, prove, try.*
Using the concordance is a skill and you must practice if you are going to develop this skill. This is the end of this chapter. May the Lord richly bless your study.

No. 58 YOUR ANSWER: *Young's.* Right. Now continue to keep record of your steps so if you are interrupted you can find your place. If you are trying to locate a verse, there are two steps to remember: Step 1, pick the most uncommon word in the verse. If you were trying to locate, "Casting all your care upon the Lord," you would not look up "Lord." There are pages of references on Lord. There are only a few for "care" or "casting." If you can't locate the verse, the probable reason is that you are misquoting the verse. Step 2, look up a synonym of the key word. If you had looked up "Lord" you would never have found this verse because it is actually "care upon him" (1 Pe 5:7), not "Lord." Suppose you want to locate a verse in your Bible that says something

like this, "Promotion doesn't come from man but from God." What is your first step in finding this verse?
—Pick the most common word. section 13
—Pick the most uncommon word. section 9

No. 59 YOUR ANSWER: *Eleven.* This is correct if you counted the times "world" is used in a phrase or translated from a phrase: WORLD (standeth, beginning of the, without end) [from the center column on p. 1074]. In these exercises we won't be talking about or using these compounds unless they are mentioned in the instructions. Count the others (Greek only) and return to section 42 and select the answer.

No. 60 YOUR ANSWER: *Strong's.* No. You cannot use this program with Strong's. Did you read the introduction to this chapter? Go back to section 52 and pick the right answer.

No. 61 YOUR ANSWER: *Changing a word from the letters of one language into the alphabet of another.* Right. Now let's take a little pop quiz to see how you are doing.
1. How many words are translated by the English word "life"? (Do not count combinations such as "life again" or "lifetime."
   Hebrew? _____ Greek? _____
2. What is the literal meaning of the word "life" used in 2 Ti 2:4 according to the concordance? _____
3. What is the literal meaning of the word "life" used in Luke 9:24? _____
4. What is the transliterated spelling of the word that is translated "life" in John 1:4? _____
5. Is the Greek word translated "life" in John 10:15 ever translated by any other English words? _____ If so, list the other English words. _____
6. Is the same Greek word used for "life" in John 10:10 and John 10:15? _____
7. What is the transliterated spelling for the word "life" used in Matthew 6:25? _____
8. Is the same Greek word used for "believe" in John 3:16 and John 3:36? _____

123

9. What is the literal meaning of the word translated "world" in Matthew 28:20? _____
10. Is the Greek word translated "prove" in Romans 12:2 ever translated by any other English words? _____ If so, list them. _____

When you have finished, check your work with section 57.

No. 62 YOUR ANSWER: *Look in the main concordance.* Correct. The references will be divided by the different words that are translated "prayer." A Hebrew or Greek word will often be translated by more than one English word. How can you know what these words are and how many ways they are translated?

    —By looking up the Greek or Hebrew word
       in the main part of the concordance.   section 56
    —By looking up the Greek or Hebrew word
       in the lexicon on the back.   section 65

No. 63 YOUR ANSWER: *7.* This was listed on page 209. The reflexive stem example in Young's prefatory note was "he killed himself." The action comes back upon or in behalf of the subject. Deuteronomy 5:21 means "Neither shalt thou covet [for yourself] thy neighbour's wife." In Genesis 24:65 the verb translated "covered herself" is also reflexive and is another example (it is also entered on p. 209 in the concordance). How many of the following references have "covet" as a number 7 (reflexive)? Joshua 7:21; Acts 20:33; Habakkuk 2:9, Proverbs 21:26. When you have your answer, turn to section 51.

No. 64 YOUR ANSWER: *Proverbs 3:35.* You are wrong. Did you look this up in your Bible? Go back to section 20 and pick the correct answer.

No. 65 YOUR ANSWER: *By looking up the Greek or Hebrew word in the lexicon in the back.* Correct. It will also have a number after each different translation to tell the times it has been translated with that word.

124

Transliteration and translation are often confused. Which of the following is a definition for transliteration?

—Changing a word from the letters of one
language into the alphabet of another.   section 61

—Changing a word from one language into
the word(s) of another language.   section 69

No. 66 YOUR ANSWER: *They are not verbs.* Yes they are. Review section 48 and then go on to section 68.

No. 67 YOUR ANSWER: *Look in the lexicons in the back.* No, you have it backward. Return to section 55 and pick the right answer.

No. 68 YOUR ANSWER: *Kal or number 1.* Correct. If a number is not given, it is a number 1. This means the subject is doing the acting (1, 3, and 5 are actives, while 2, 4, and 6 are passives). The subject is acted upon in a passive. A number 1 is also the simple stem. If the author wanted to indicate stronger action, he would have used the intensive stem (number 3 in the active or number 4 in the passive). Young's example in the prefatory note is "he killed violently." When the author wants to show cause, and, usually by its very nature, strong action, the causitive stems are used (number 5 in the active and number 6 in the passive). Often the word "cause" can be introduced into the translation. Using the word "prepare," fill out the following chart:

Reference	Voice	Stem	Expanded paraphrase
			"even [cause] to
2 Chronicles 2:9	active	5	prepare"
Isaiah 30:33			
Psalm 23:5			
Jeremiah 6:4			
Jeremiah 12:3			
Psalm 59:4			

When you have checked these, turn to section 55. Do the work! You will never learn if you don't try.

No. 69 YOUR ANSWER: *Changing a word from one language into the word(s) of another language.* No, you have them confused. Return to section 65.

18

Suggested Bible-Study Tools

While the emphasis of this book is upon personal Bible study, there are some basic tools that will be of great value. The following books are recommended because of the aid that they will give in the study of the Bible itself and their permanent value in your library:

BIBLE VERSIONS

King James Version
New American Standard Bible
The Amplified Bible
New International Version
The New Testament in the Language of the People by Charles B. Williams
The New Testament: An Expanded Translation by Kenneth S. Wuest

CONCORDANCES

Young, Robert. *Young's Analytical Concordance to the Bible*. Grand Rapids: Eerdmans, 1955.

BIBLE DICTIONARY

Unger, Merrill F. *Unger's Bible Dictionary*. Chicago: Moody, 1957.

BIBLE GEOGRAPHY

Aharoni, Yohanan, and Avi-yonah, Michael. *The Macmillan Bible Atlas*. New York: Macmillan, 1968.

Pfeiffer, Charles F., and Vos, Howard F. *The Wycliffe Historical Geography of Bible Lands*. Chicago: Moody, 1967.

ONE-VOLUME COMMENTARIES
OF THE ENTIRE BIBLE

Guthrie, D., et al., eds. *The New Bible Commentary: Revised*. Grand Rapids: Eerdmans, 1970.

Pfeiffer, Charles F., and Harrison, Everett F., eds. *The Wycliffe Bible Commentary*. Chicago: Moody, 1962.

Unger, Merrill F. *Unger's Bible Handbook*. Chicago: Moody, 1966.

WORD STUDIES

Girdlestone, Robert B. *Synonyms of the Old Testament*. Grand Rapids: Eerdmans, 1948.

Vine, W. E. *An Expository Dictionary of New Testament Words*. Old Tappan, N.J.: Revell, 1940.

Wuest, Kenneth S. *Word Studies in the Greek New Testament*. Grand Rapids: Eerdmans, 1973. Available in three clothbound volumes or in fourteen paperback volumes.

HARMONIES

Goodwin, Frank J. *A Harmony of the Life of St. Paul*. Grand Rapids: Baker, 1951.

Robertson, A. T. *A Harmony of the Gospels*. New York: Harper & Row, 1922.

OTHER BOOKS BY THE AUTHOR

Baughman, Ray E. *The Abundant Life*. Chicago: Moody, 1959. Also available in Spanish.

_____. *Bible History Visualized*. Chicago: Moody, 1963.

_____. *The Kingdom of God Visualized*. Chicago: Moody, 1972.

_____. *The Life of Christ Visualized*. Chicago: Moody, 1968.